RESPONSIBLE?
HELL NO!

DANIEL MIKLOS KOLOS

BALBOA.PRESS
A DIVISION OF HAY HOUSE

Balboa Press books may be ordered through booksellers or by contacting:

Balboa Press
A Division of Hay House
1663 Liberty Drive
Bloomington, IN 47403
www.balboapress.com
1 (877) 407-4847

Because of the dynamic nature of the Internet, any web addresses or links contained in this book may have changed since publication and may no longer be valid. The views expressed in this work are solely those of the author and do not necessarily reflect the views of the publisher, and the publisher hereby disclaims any responsibility for them.

The author of this book does not dispense medical advice or prescribe the use of any technique as a form of treatment for physical, emotional, or medical problems without the advice of a physician, either directly or indirectly. The intent of the author is only to offer information of a general nature to help you in your quest for emotional and spiritual well-being. In the event you use any of the information in this book for yourself, which is your constitutional right, the author and the publisher assume no responsibility for your actions.

Any people depicted in stock imagery provided by Getty Images are models, and such images are being used for illustrative purposes only.
Certain stock imagery © Getty Images.

Scripture taken from the King James Version of the Bible.

Print information available on the last page.

ISBN: 978-1-9822-3513-0 (sc)
ISBN: 978-1-9822-3515-4 (hc)
ISBN: 978-1-9822-3514-7 (e)

Library of Congress Control Number: 2019914357

Balboa Press rev. date: 11/07/2019

CONTENTS

ACKNOWLEDGEMENT

In 2014 Dr. Gabor Mate held a one-day workshop in Owen Sound, Ontario, Canada. A dear friend had to drag me, protesting, resisting and denying that I have anything to do with addiction. She bought me Dr. Mate's book, *In the Realm of Hungry Ghosts,* which opened my eyes.

Dr. Mate 'spoke my language.' I don't just mean that he was a fellow Hungarian. No. Every sentence he spoke turned out to be meaningful for me. The lecture hall was filled with professional mental health workers. I am sure there were other 'lay' people like me, but I felt no deficit at all. Not a single one of these people, from psychiatrists to hot-shot therapists and addiction specialists had any idea what was coming. In fact, having read the popular book on childhood brain development, *The Magical Child*, written in 1978 by Joseph Chilton Pearce, I had far more knowledge about how trauma interrupts brain development than most people in the lecture hall.

Dr. Mate came to Owen Sound, Ontario, because Sat Dharam Kaur, N.D. had invited him. She had just developed a holistic teaching program called Beyond Addiction. Having read Dr. Mate's book on addiction, she saw a perfect fit. She enhanced her program with his knowledge about addiction. Sat Dharam Kaur had combined a basic Life-Coach teaching with Kundalini Yoga and the teaching of Yogi Bhajan, with holistic health practices, including specific food and supplementation for various body cleanses, and finally with the latest scientific research on brain development.

At that event, I asked Sat Dharam Kaur 'what is the next step?' In April, 2014 I enrolled in her Beyond Addiction Program. At the same time, she had convinced Dr. Mate to create a workshop series based on his studies and experiences with addicts and trauma. At first, he was reluctant. "I don't have anything to teach," he thought. A series of workshops in Vancouver and Toronto changed his mind. Even though he thought nobody would show up, he consistently filled lecture halls with 360 or more people. He claimed that you cannot help others reach their pain and learn to cope with their painful emotions until you face and accept your own pain. Wherever we are in our emotional development is exactly the point where we can bring others.

I was present for the two Toronto Workshops called Compassionate Inquiry. I took the opportunity to sign up and participate in two more series of on-line workshops with Dr. Mate, then asked Sat Dharam Kaur's permission to study and practice for a Compassionate Inquiry Certification course she had organized from Dr. Mate's workshop series. Instead of having 'nothing to say,' Gabor Mate found himself at the forefront of a therapeutic revolution that starts with the practitioner: if the Practitioner can get in touch with his or her pain, then so can any client that wants—or needs—to!

INTRODUCTION

Part 1 Where Do I Begin?

Anywhere. Every page in this book is relevant to something I do, something I have done, or something I have observed. I may begin reading anywhere. This book is created in such a way, that I may pick it up, read a chapter, skip to another, and so forth. It is meant to support me on my very individual journey.

Where I begin may be due to my personality-type. How redundant! On the one hand there are perfectionists, administrators, categorizers; on the other, anti-authoritarians, creatives, free spirits.

The march of psychological and neurobiological research keeps uncovering simpler and more effective standards of emotional health and therapies. Judith Lewis Herman, a Harvard psychiatrist, wrote a book called *Trauma and Recovery* in 1995. Basically she said that there is only one psychiatric diagnosis, and everything else is just a variation on this theme. She called this diagnosis "Complex Post Traumatic Stress."

Since then, psychiatrists continued to find and name more and more personality dysfunctions (whether or not they were aware that all dysfunctions developed from a series of childhood traumas) for which drug companies have developed new psychotropic medications.

Personality, within this evolutionary context, is a defense mechanism we pick up, or adapt, as small, pre-verbal children, every time one of our needs is not met. In one sense, we develop a personality every time our brain development is interrupted both in the womb and as pre-verbal infants and toddlers. These interruptions are not our fault! At that age we are not responsible for these developments.

Hardly anyone escapes these early emotional (pre-verbal) responses to apparent survival issues. The mother's ordinary stresses and strains replace oxytocin and serotonin (two feel-good hormones) in her bloodstream with adrenalin and cortisol (two hormones that are connected to stress levels and distress in the body). It is completely natural.

In the uterus, however, this hormonal exchange becomes a survival issue for the gestating child. The repeated loss of the feel-good hormones stresses the fetus. It is 'interpreted' by the fetus, in its emerging sensitivity, as a potential threat to its life.

Our survival responses are few: fight, flight or freeze. The fetus can kick its legs, flail its arms, but the most common response is for the fetus to freeze—to go into a trance! In this stress-induced trance, while the fetus waits for the oxytocin and serotonin to return, it stops developing. The loss of connection to its emotional development creates trauma.

There is nothing the mother can do about encountering the stresses of everyday life. It is not the mother's fault that the developing fetus is acquiring this trauma. It is simply the natural process that occurs within the womb. However, that trauma stays with us as we move through our lives.

This book is about how that repeated trauma plays us, drives us, and preoccupies us for the rest of our lives.

INTRODUCTION

Part 2 There is Only One Diagnosis: "Trauma"

You will notice that I often write in the first person here, because as you read this book, I want to welcome you to see yourself as that "I". There is hardly any human interaction, from personal relationships to group dynamics, where individuals are free of self-consciousness, limiting judgments, resentments, fears, anger or insecurities.

This book is a testament to how I came to recognize the influences that seized me in childhood and drove me, unconsciously and irresponsibly, into middle age and on, until I came into synch with these methods of self-awareness.

Recognizing trauma and facing pain and learning to cope with it is not an 'age-related' thing. For instance, there are self-confident teenagers who, when they are put down or insulted, see that the words coming at them have nothing to do with them. The nasty words, the bullying, the pain, belong to the one who let these loose in the first place to soothe his or her own pain.

So, wherever I am on this journey, at whatever age, I am in the right place, and right on track.

I just begin where I am.

As we go along together, see if you recognize me.

In other words, see if you can recognize yourself in this book.

"I Am Not Held; Therefore, I Am Not Loved."

The most basic human need, after being fed, is connection. It is being connected to the one who feeds me.

As a newborn, I don't have memory. I only have needs. When I lose touch with the one who feeds me, I also lose touch with my source of food. This is about my survival.

The hippocampus, the organ in the brain that regulates memory, is still developing when we are infants and toddlers. Some researchers say that it becomes fully functional at the age of four.

Does that mean I can't remember anything until I reach that age? No! Let's just say memory development differs slightly for everyone. However, these very early traumas do stay with us.

Unfortunately, it is normal to experience stress due to survival issues in early childhood. While not being held by the mother is a survival issue for any infant, for a two-or four-year-old child, it becomes a negative learning process. I develop beliefs such as "I am not held; therefore, I am not worthy" and "I am not held; therefore, no matter how much I cry, I am not going to be heard."

As a child, when I am not held by my parents, I give up. I begin to believe that expressing my emotions is not working, because I am not being held, and not having my needs met. As that child, I still need connection: I need to be held.

What strategies are open to me? I am in trouble. First, my strategic brain has not even developed yet! Secondly, my survival instincts can unconsciously suppress whatever emotion arises.

These survival instincts are the drivers of my earliest adaptations. A survival threat, and my response to it, begins to shape me as a person. It is a process of repressed emotions that begins to define my personality. I will carry that repressed fear, anger, or withdrawal throughout my adult life. I will not heal because no one in this world will hold me twenty-four/seven.

Am I out of my mind? There is practically no one in the so-called civilized world who feels they have to hold their newborn child twenty-four/seven for the first two or three years of their life! Women would never consent to bearing children if they knew they would have to have this level of commitment to their newborn babies! Maternity leave would need to last for four years.

No. This does not happen in our current society.

"I Am Not Held, Therefore, I Am Not Loved."

Part 2

Can billions of people be wrong?
Yes.

Joseph Chilton Pearce wrote a book called *The Magical Child,* back in 1977. Neurobiological research and psychiatric interpretation had already accepted that the first nine months of human life is the "in-arms" period, which is the time when it is most important for a child to be held.

Lack of being held causes a separation between my developing consciousness and my authentic emotions. Another way of saying that is this: I separate myself from experiencing my own authentic emotions in order to attract my food-provider's attention. This constant maneuvering for lost contact stops my own emotional development. My separation from my own emotional development remains my basic trauma all my life—but unconsciously. The coping mechanisms I develop become my personality.

In the process, the suppressed fear, pain, and belief, all of which accompany the trauma, continue to live in me. And I keep acting them out subconsciously. The only escape available for me is to find a way to reconnect to my lost and undeveloped emotional self as an adult. These separations have caused a deep pain that needs to be released. Reconnection in my adulthood allows me to cope with the painful trauma that my early survival issues have formed. In a sense, reconnection washes away the long-carried pain in a way that is similar to the way water soaks the chemical out of every seed—the chemical that keeps the seed from sprouting!

My Story, Part 1

What Happened: The Facts

When I was four years old, my parents went to a resort for a week and dropped me off at my grandparents' apartment. This was in post-World War II Budapest.

I adored my grandmother. She had taken care of me for most of my life and was my ally when my mother was out of sorts. My grandfather was a shell-shocked World War I hero. He coped with his pain by drinking too much *slivovitz pálinka,* a distilled plum brandy he called a "heart strengthener."

Upon my arrival for this visit, they immediately asked the neighbors to send their four-year-old daughter over to be my playmate. The neighbors were delighted. My grandfather took us across the street to the Ludovika Gardens. He sat on a bench and conversed with other men while the little girl and I climbed the low-branched trees and found comfortable seats across from each other. It was a warm summer, and all we wore were white cotton underpants.

Before long, I began to imitate other preschool boys I had seen on previous visits to the park. They would pull one side of their underpants up when girls passed by with their grandparents. When I did that, my new friend giggled. Then she pulled up one side of her panties. This time, I giggled. My grandfather looked up, but by then all was back in place.

The week passed with lots of visits to the park. One cloudy day, we remained in my grandparents' apartment. The little girl and I decided to get married. We didn't know anything about sex, or romance. All we knew was that adults discouraged us from looking at each other's genitals. Of course, this made us curious. And our idea of marriage was that once you married someone, you were allowed to do that.

We entered my grandparents' large, Victorian bathroom together. In the dim light of a single light bulb, we ceremonially took off our underpants, held hands, and walked up and down the bathroom looking at each other's genitals.

We were solemn and quiet.

Perhaps wanting to use the bathroom, or perhaps looking for us, my grandmother suddenly entered the bathroom. She took one look at us and contorted her face. She began to yell and scream insults at me. She took a hold of me and spanked me. She made us put our underpants back on and then sent my friend back home. I was never allowed to see her again.

My Story, Part 2

The Feelings, Interpretations, and Consequent Beliefs

My world was shattered. My grandmother—my friend and ally—had turned on me. I felt betrayed. Betrayal, however, is an interpretation. When I told this story in two separate Compassionate Inquiry therapy sessions, I could not "feel" an actual feeling associated with my relationship with my grandmother. However, I could feel shame and humiliation from receiving the beating in front of that little girl.

That day, I went back into the living room where my grandfather was sitting. When I started telling him what happened in between my sobbing, my grandmother yelled and screamed at him as well, and accused him of being the cause of it all. At that time I had no idea why she would accuse him in that way. But now I know that my grandmother was not upset about what I was doing. She lost her temper and control because of what had happened to her at the hands of my grandfather. As an adult, my mother told me about all the terrible abuse, pain, and humiliation my grandmother had to endure during her marriage to my grandfather.

One lifelong response that became clear from this incident was that every time I found myself in an intimate situation with a woman, I was expecting to be punished—even with my wife. I expected to be punished even when I had done nothing wrong!

CHAPTER

5

Connecting with My Anger

My second Compassionate Inquiry practitioner did not let me get away with just interpreting what had happened in that Victorian bathroom. She insisted that I stay with the feelings I'd had immediately following the beating in the bathroom. I did and I became very emotional; my entire body buzzed. Tears came to my eyes.

In spite of these body sensations, no words came to my mind, so my practitioner changed tactics. She asked me, "As an adult, reflecting back upon being beaten for innocently playing house with a little girl, what would you say?"

I had an immediate response.

"WTF?"

The practitioner became enthusiastic.

"Exactly! Now say it three more times, and say it as if you meant it!"

So I did.

"How do you feel now?" my practitioner asked.

I said, "I feel good!"

"Yes," she said, "you feel good now, but how does that child feel inside you?"

I felt nothing.

The practitioner had to prompt me. "Would not that child feel peeved?"

It was only then that the word *angry* came into my mind. I said, "I felt angry! I would have had every right to feel angry!" Then slowly, in shock, I began to feel these waves of anger and pain wash over me.

My anger was so repressed that for seventy years I would brag that there was no anger in me. Yet every two or three years, I would inexplicably explode into a fit of anger!

The Compassionate Inquiry practice continued to prepare my adult mind to accept my four-year-old child's pain and anger, to develop healthy and useful coping mechanisms, and to reconnect that repressed memory to my developing authenticity.

If I Feel Bad, It's My Fault!

Life is radiant. I radiate what I feel into my environment. I am like an antenna in that I constantly transmit my feelings—or my mood—to my partners, my children, my dogs and cats, my colleagues at the workplace, and even to my vehicles and the roads I use.

There is nothing wrong with feeling bad. It is a normal part of a cycle that I keep going through. There is nothing "good" and "bad" about feeling bad. It is part of a normal cycle. What is "bad," however, is when I take my feelings out on the people and animals around me; when I begin to smash china, break furniture and punch my first through the wall. These reactions-or consequences-of feeling bad are actually signs of unresolved childhood trauma. The problem is that nobody tells me what is making me feel bad. Hardly anyone actually teaches us to make the connection to the cause. Why is that? Because emotional trauma is a relatively new concept. Historically, it is only now that emotional trauma as a treatable-or resolvable-condition has hit the streets, as it were.

I seldom complain when I feel good. But sometimes I do complain when I feel bad. It's normal to want feeling bad to end. One thing is certain! a bad feeling will change.

I had to be taught to pay attention to myself a little bit; to become aware. As a result, my first line of defense against feeling bad is to breathe deeply and listen to my breath.

A part of being human is that we like to name and measure things. Just how bad I can feel cannot be measured. Can I name my feeling? I used to avoid it at all costs! Instead, I give it a moniker: "I am depressed." "I am abandoned." "I feel let down." "I feel betrayed!"

Yet none of these are feelings. These monikers are perceptions.

Another line of approach I use is that I reason out my feelings. "I feel bad; therefore, I am depressed." "The love of my life left me, and I feel abandoned." "My colleagues did not support my idea, and I feel let down."

Now I think I know my feelings.

Do I? No!

I Love You! Why Don't You Love Me Too?

There is no question that 'love' is a feeling! However, saying/feeling "I love you" can be giving or taking. On the 'giving' side, the difference between "I love baked beans" and "I love another person" is, of course a matter of intensity.

On the taking side, however, I sometimes use the phrase "I love you" in order to get something I want or need. For instance when I say. "I love you" and what I mean is "I want sex with you,", this is lust. There is nothing wrong with lust, of course, as long as I admit to it. Admitting my lust also helps me to find a partner who will reciprocate; a partner who is willing to work with me. Lust in action is hard, passionate work. It is not love. In this case, I am just using the word 'love' to get something.

If I love you, why does it happen that you don't love me?

This is a dangerous question, as I simply cannot know why another person will not love me. I can and must ask, but the answer is not in the other person. The answer is within me. And it can lead me to some damaging beliefs.

Am I going through life believing that "I am not lovable?"

A more pertinent question is, "How much do I love myself?"

If I love you and I don't love myself, I am projecting from an empty shell. When I go to the movies and watch a film, both the projector and the screen are inanimate, unfeeling objects. The movie, itself, is an illusion into which I willingly enter and willingly suspend my disbelief.

Do I want to enter a relationship with another human being on the basis of suspending my disbelief? Have I fallen in love with an illusion?

Well, YES! If I don't love myself, then I am an empty shell. If I don't love myself, then I don't have to feel responsible for myself.

Sometimes the illusion is easier.

Can I Love Myself?

Part One: Self-Love

Self-love is a term packed with all kinds of "dangerous" possible meanings, but it is totally worth discussing.

When I hear the term, "self-love", I may jump directly to the label, 'that one is then narcissistic'. Narcissism (the pursuit of gratification from <u>vanity</u> or <u>egotistic</u> admiration of one's idealized <u>self image</u> and attributes) is fascinating and most of us indulge in it to some degree. Narcissism becomes a problem for me to the degree that I am, or am not aware of it. *Being aware* of myself is very much key (for more on this, see chapters 38-41.) If I become deeply narcissistic and I lose my awareness, I am in trouble. If I do not grow out of this dysfunction naturally, I should be treated by a qualified psychotherapist. Alternatively, I could seek to become aware of my personality and my internal processes and change it for myself.

'Self-love' has also become a euphemism for masturbation. There is nothing wrong with masturbation as long as it does not become an obsessive-compulsive drive. Masturbation is often hormone-driven. However, it is also environmentally driven. In the spring when reproduction among insects, plants and some animals comes to a crescendo, there is no way a human being can avoid getting caught up in the spirit of the season.

Well, perhaps there is!

With the help of my social conditioning, I may have repressed my sexual feelings to such a secretive place that I walk around in public with a big, invisible flag declaring to all who can see: "I am asexual."

There is good reason for sexual repression. Most of us grow up (or have grown up) with adults, teachers, religious persons and other role models who either practiced celibacy or pretended to. These adults usually teach us all about how wrong and bad sex and sexuality is. As a child, even into adolescence, I believed that every adult (my teachers) lived and spoke their truth. Their truth, however, may not be my need. And the real truth is that they were preaching to us to, "Do as I say, not as I do."

When I exit a particularly sexy movie, my hormonal drive is in high gear. I am preoccupied with having access to that sexual satisfaction I just saw other people enjoy on screen. Most of the time, I cannot get it. Instead, I am either disappointed, or I masturbate.

Even with our technological advances, my options are the same. After a bout of 'sexting' (exchanging provocative or graphic sexual comments by texting on a cell-phone or any mobile contraption) the brain, and especially my imagination, is determined to reproduce that sexual satisfaction. If I don't have a readily available and willing partner at that moment of heightened lust, repressing my sexuality is one unconscious route to take. Masturbation is another, healthier, option.

In one sense, anything that brings me a moment's pleasure is 'self-love'. The danger lies in crossing the line from pleasure to addiction.

Can I Love Myself?

Part 2: Self-Care

Self-Love is when I am good to myself.

Self-love is a balancing act between narcissism at one end of the pendulum, perfect balance around the centre, and co-dependency (the notion that I can't be okay unless I am pleasing others, or my emotions are tied to theirs) at the other end.

Not surprisingly, I want the balance. I am good to myself (practice self-care) when I get a good night's sleep. It can be that simple.

I practice self-care when I skip breakfast and eat a fresh salad with a high protein main course and no sugar. (I am referring to my 'current' "ketogenic" diet, which may only be a passing fad.)

I practice self-care when I go to the gym and work out, or go for a walk or run, and get a massage.

I practice self-care when I let myself be surprised by not planning a day or a weekend, and go out and see what happens. When I do this, it is without expectations or fears. It's just 'me', as a neutral observer who judges neither myself, nor those I watch. I allow non-verbal communications to happen from my essence to my environment, whatever that may mean—from whatever place I am in. There are no winners, and no losers. There is no stress in that moment.

Is this a pipe-dream? No. Just a possibility.

When I discussed the idea of "self-love" with friends who also struggled with this concept and practice, one of them said, "I can't go around telling myself 'I love myself' day in and day out. That would be ludicrous!"

I asked, "Would it?"

In order to make the question a practical one, rather than a theoretical one, I began a forty-day trial period of practicing self-love and challenged my friends to try it as well.

*Web*MD* points out that when adult children of alcoholic parents tried to sense their self-worth, all they could think about was how they were treated as though they were not worthy of their parents' time, their love, and their affection. This was true, even though this had taken place fifty years ago. We have since then accomplished so much, blossomed as creative people, as organizers and administrators. Some of us even stand out in our community. We are so worth it!

*(https://www.webmd.com/sex-relationships/features/signs-of-a-codependent-relationship#1)

I did my forty days of saying to myself, "I love myself!" daily, as often as I could think of it. That was three years ago. It felt odd at first, and even artificial. At times I didn't believe that I was being genuine. The others in this small group agreed with me. All but one dropped the practice. But the saying grew on me. My own take-away on this 'experiment' was this: I love myself and by loving myself, I feel totally worthy to love you.

CHAPTER

10

Can I Love Myself?

Part 3: What Are the Boundaries of Addiction?

I don't know. I just recognize addiction when I see it—mostly in others, sometimes in myself. This is what I see: a constant repetition of a pleasurable action that I crave and cannot stop, that in the long run, is potentially self-harming.

Gabor Maté, a physician who worked with addicts at Vancouver's notorious East Side, an enclave of addicts, for 17 years, is adamant that addiction is not a disease. He observed that addiction is a coping mechanism that signals deeply held beliefs about one's self; that these beliefs are repressed, and, therefore, are unresolved emotional trauma. He believes that it is not the addiction that needs to be treated. What needs to be treated, rather, is the pain that the addiction purportedly soothes. The pain, in turn, is not about what happened. The pain is about how what happened caused a disconnection from the addict's authentic self-during childhood!

This much more inclusive diagnosis means treatment for the addiction is possible by helping the "addict", or, rather, the emotionally disconnected person, become aware that their addiction can be emotionally resolved.

The question is, how is that original trauma resolved?

If unresolved emotional trauma tend to trigger (cause) addiction, there are no boundaries. Every human being has experienced emotional trauma, and we are not responsible for our original traumas! This knowledge can help to alleviate the guilt often experienced by addicts who seek help, only to be told that their behavior is all their fault and a damage to themselves and others. Thus, I can be healed without inflicting more damage.

One of the first things an infant learns whenever his or her primary caretaker (usually the mother) leaves, is that "I am not lovable." Of course, it is not a verbal development, but rather an inner survival instinct. This survival instinct creates the child's disconnection from his/her authentic self and produces the child's loss of self-love and self-compassion! That self-love has to be reintroduced in order to resolve its loss.

If the parent does not hold the child; if the parent does not acknowledge the child's pain; if the parent remains unconscious of the child's loss of connection to its authentic self, unresolved trauma develops and remains throughout our lives. Some of us successfully repress our trauma and live with the constant pain. Others wonder why they cannot maintain a loving relationship. Many soothe their pain with a plethora of addictions.

Unresolved traumas tend to attract addictions.

Can I Love Myself?

Part 4: Resolving the Loss of Self-Love

The most often cited childhood trauma is absent parents. "I felt abandoned!" Yet, 'abandonment' is not a feeling. It is a state of being. A person might say, "as a child, I remember clinging to my father's trouser legs every morning when he left for work and begging him to stay."

'Abandonment,' therefore, is a misnomer. The conditions, which the child experiences, are 'not being heard,' and 'not being valued.' However, neither of these—not being heard nor valued—are feelings! These concepts will develop into the child's belief system throughout his or her life.

A psychotherapist can explore these unconscious beliefs with me, and in the process I may find the actual feelings connected to these experiences. Perceptions, such as 'abandonment', and beliefs, such as "I am not heard, therefore, I am not worthy," are layers that tend to hide our feelings.

There are times when the last thing I want to do is to find and face my feelings!

Therapy, or self-analysis, may lead to a deep fear of death. Why fear of death? As a pre-verbal child, or a three-to-four-year-old you had survival instincts that translated into a fear of death: "if a parent leaves me, I will not be fed and I will die." Unresolved trauma means that I, as the adult, have not yet resolved that trauma. Even as an adult, I am still unconsciously function under its spell.

While I am a child, that fear is justified. Every child is totally dependent upon its parents for its survival. Childhood attachment, therefore, is a natural (and necessary) condition, or state of being.

Dr. Maté talks about resolving a child's fear of abandonment in this way, and I paraphrase him: 'If you have to drop your child off at daycare every morning, hug your child, and say, "I love you!" And reassure your child that you will come back. It teaches the child that 'yes, the pain of separation is real, but there is a resolution: father/mother will return. The child learns not just to cope with its pain, but to accept it.'

Such a repeated assurance will allow the child to resolve his or her own trauma.

I Don't Ask. I am Afraid of Being Rejected.

Right! Me and ninety-nine percent of all people. What's the real problem? It could be the question I ask. So let's just look at one. If I go up to people and ask "will you have sex with me?" then I am bound to be rejected.

OK, so that is an extreme example! Most of my questions are really mundane, like "should I take a laxative, Doctor, or just eat more fiber?" My problem is that I may not dare to ask that question even though there is no rejection involved. I can resolve this question by making an intelligent choice without advice! My reluctance to ask however may happen because I may find it embarrassing.

The majority of things I want to ask are about personal relationships (Would you like to go on a date with me?) or personal gain (Would you do me a favor?) The probability of a favorable answer to these questions is 50/50.

Students in school will quite often not ask most of the questions that come to their minds. These are questions that should be asked. These are perfectly appropriate questions. What is the reason for not asking? Lack of confidence; "what will 'they' think of me?" or "that's probably a stupid question." To be blunt, these questions are not asked because, as that student I am afraid to ask.

As an adult, if I ask my boss, "Can I switch to the other department? I feel I can improve my performance and my usefulness to the company there," this question offers a standard that is a long-held value among self-confident people. It offers the "Most Beneficial Outcome," or MBO.

What is MBO? It is a win-win-win situation. It is almost rejection-proof. An MBO is beneficial to me, it is beneficial for my immediate environment (including my boss), and it is beneficial to the whole, the ecology, the economy, even the Universe. Expressing gratitude, saying "Thank you!" for a small favor is an MBO.

If I have a Big Idea that sparks a vision quest, and this Big Idea is a win-win-win situation that will make me rich, make my associates rich, and in every way enrich the greater society and the environment, people will flock to me to work on such a project. Or they will search their minds/hearts to find their own vision quest, and create even more of a win for the whole culture.

If I don't ask in the first place, it is because I have a belief system in place that keeps me from asking. That belief system hides my feeling of fear. It is not you, or my boss, that I am afraid of. That feeling of fear developed in my early childhood. I have carried it ever since I first became disconnected from my authentic self, but I have been unaware of it all this time.

My Story

Part 1: The Facts: University College, University of Pennsylvania

Looking back, recalling my 'history', having explicit memory, and all the benefits of hindsight allow me to piece together this portion of the unconscious dream-walk that was my life.

When I was in high school, I was chatty with all my teachers. Or, perhaps, they were chatty with me. All I knew is that they all saw 'great potential' in me, and my job was to fulfill their expectations.

I was eighteen and I had earned a four-year scholarship, plus stipend to a 'whiskey' university. I was off to seek that potential.

At University College, I knew no one and no one knew me. Sure, I had an assigned roommate, and I participated in endless corridor debates about religion and politics. I had a Guidance counselor whom I saw only once. When it came time to "choose a major", I had to ask my roommate what a 'major' was. (See Chapter 61 for this 'story' in a different context)

I participated in classroom discussions about my assignments, and I became somewhat familiar with the professors, but I was not one to ask questions. All I wanted to do was to pass each course so that I could keep my scholarship. And I did that.

Even back then, I considered myself to be a fairly intelligent and knowledgeable person, and I already had some pretensions about wisdom. But at the end of the four years of college, the only person with whom I had actual conversations, was my senior thesis advisor, and my part-time employer. the former congratulated me on my graduation, saying "You are now able to read the New York Times-and understand it!"

During those four years, it is possible that I did not ask a single question in any of my classes.

It is not that I did anything wrong. It is not that I would have done it differently. What makes this story relevant to me is the fine line between my illusions and my delusions. (See Chapter 20)

My Story

Part 2: What Happened? The Feelings, Interpretations, and the Consequent Beliefs

I did not talk with my professors privately. I did not ask them questions in class, unless it pertained to homework due. It was not ego that stopped me. It was abject fear. I felt a self-degrading fear of authority. Unconsciously, I very likely expected to be punished.

That my professors represented authority figures, made sense to me. My father came across as a know-it-all in line with the German-Hungarian hierarchical tradition. The father was the head of the family and he knew everything. Not only did father know everything, he was always right. And, he was never challenged.

There is one more nugget to this dysfunctional picture, as well.

Father had the right to punish.

This role might not have been very different from English, French or even American post-World-War-II standards. "Spare the rod and spoil the child," wherever practiced, meant that whether or not the child understood the 'crime', punishment was administered anyway. Punishment, in my case, was proportional to my father's satisfaction.

One can get used to spanking or beating, but to 'get used to' punishment means a certain set of emotional shut-downs. Chances are that I was able to get used to it, because I had repressed my survival instincts. I was afraid when my father was in a certain 'mood', but none of us knew about trauma, and certainly not PTSD. My father, like millions of other laborers and soldiers and traumatized civilians who survived the war and the death camps, suffered all his life from it.

How did I feel? I have no idea. I had repressed my fear. But there were definite interpretations that came with these beatings.

One of them was the thought that, "I deserved to be beaten."

My mother could not protect me from my father's rages and so I felt alone, and vulnerable.

This is how I formed a set of beliefs about myself. No matter what I do, I cannot please my father, so I am worthless. No matter what I do, I cannot get my father to love me, therefore I am unlovable. On top of all that, because of my failure to win my father's love, I felt guilty!

These interpretations and beliefs, of course, were not verbalized. I was not conscious of any of it until recently. I knew that story, and I even resented my father, but I had no idea what the trauma was doing to me.

Due to the Hungarian Revolutions of October 23, 1956, my mother, sister and I escaped Hungary. My father, who was 16 years older than my mother, decided to remain in Hungary. In his opinion, Western society did not respect people over 50, unless they were rich. So he stayed.

He might have been right on that one!

My mother divorced my father and went on with her life. Throughout my life, I used to brag that I also divorced my father. I believed that leaving him, back in 1956 was the best thing I ever did in my life!

What is a Belief System?

Part 1: The Personal: How Did I Get a Belief System in the First Place?

Am I responsible for my beliefs? Hell no!!!

As Carolyn Myss wrote in her book, *The Anatomy of Spirit*, we are stuffed full of beliefs between birth and age 7, or until we develop the ability to discriminate between right and wrong. Carolyn did not use these words, but she pointed out that our first, or root Chakra, is the recipient of all our primal beliefs. She called them our "tribal instructions." She is among millions of wise voices who urge us to examine our belief systems to see which of these early beliefs are still useful now that we are adults. Which of our pre-verbal beliefs are outdated, useless or intrusive?

What is a belief? It is our identity. Yes, my name is also an identity, because I believe I am "Daniel". But if I believe that I am worthless and useless, then these beliefs also become part of my identity.

Many things happened during my childhood, which confirmed, or proved to me that I was worthless and useless. My father repeated that mantra rant after rant for years. Whether I wanted them or not, those words worked themselves into my identity. When I was a student and I had a question to ask, I did not ask because I didn't think I was worth the teacher's time to give me an answer. "My Story" in chapter 13 describes this situation.

That is what a belief does. It transfers itself from one situation to another. Beliefs, fears and unresolved emotional trauma act like contagious diseases. Everything and everyone becomes tainted by the unconscious lens through which I am looking.

Obviously, when I was in school, I was not in the presence of my father. At home, though, my father found me distracting to his work. He called me useless and worthless, even after I 'divorced' him and changed continents. Though he remained in Budapest when my mother took me to the US, these beliefs came with me! As a teenager and young adult I believed all authority figures would find me useless and worthless.

The question is not whether a belief is true or false. The sad fact is that this belief becomes my identity, and I live by it completely unconsciously. All I can hope for is to gain an insight into my core beliefs, and choose to upgrade my identity. To believe I am useless and unlovable is simply not beneficial to anyone.

What is a Belief System?

Part 2: Propaganda: The Anatomy of 'Belief'

What came first, propaganda or self-brain-washing?
Ever since civilizations turned to exercising power over others by a hierarchical leadership (whether kingship or democracy with a President/Prime Minister), their two primary tools were physical force (an army) and propaganda (false claims). When propaganda works and becomes a belief system that people accept as good for them, everyone is happy.

Where the propaganda doesn't work, there is opposition, alternate parties, dissent, revolution, overthrow of systems and the beginning of new propaganda. Call me a cynic, but this is what I studied at University. One only has to look at the current state of political affairs to confirm this belief.

What is a Belief System?

Part 3: How Do I Change a Belief System?

Whoever invented Mantras, or chants, was the first person to turn propaganda into a self-calming system. Every religion and spiritual practice has some form of mantra or sound that its adherents practice, from a simple repetition of "Omm" to praying with beads, or hours of chanting.

When I asked the question, "Can I say to myself 'I love myself?' that was, and is, a mantra, a self-administered propaganda which brings me good feelings. "I am happy because I can breathe!" for instance, is a far more beneficial mantra to repeat day in and day out than "What miserable weather!" or "I can't stand my mother-in-law!"

Since a belief is an identity, if all I ever do is complain about the weather, I am the one who is miserable, not just the weather!

If all I ever do is complain about how the government is stealing my wealth, I am the one who is miserable, not the government or its representatives or administrators.

If I want to feel better, I don't need to change the weather, I don't need to overthrow the government! I need to focus on something else.

It is much more beneficial to me to focus on something like my breathing, or the sense of wellbeing in a hot bath. How about the loveliness of sipping a tiny cup of espresso in an open-air café, or, sitting in my favorite armchair and repeating the mantra "I love myself!" or "I am worthy to be loved".

The boundary of happiness is what happens outside the body and what I feel inside the body. All teachers and sages, both ancient and modern, agree that outside events, by themselves, do not bring happiness. I can buy all the latest, fashionable shoes in the world, but other than feeling a short burst of satisfaction at acquiring each pair, I cannot make a dent in my 'happiness quotient.'

An inner change or accomplishment, such as upgrading a useless childhood belief into an enlightened adult, belief, is my true source of happiness.

Here is how it works.

My Story

Part 1: The Facts: How I Was Bullied in First Grade

When I was six years old and entered the first grade in school, the discipline that was enforced upon us approached a reign of terror. I had to have my desk neatly arranged so that my ink bottle, (yes, I am that old!), the blotter, the pen and the pencil, the ruler and the eraser, were each in the right place across the flat surface at the top of my desk.

At eight o'clock, sharp, the door handle would move and the teacher entered the classroom. He walked around to check each desk with a ruler in his hand. If all was well, he went to his desk and started the day with a roll-call.

Many mornings the class bully stood up ten seconds before eight o'clock, leaned over to my desk and rearranged the items or spilled the ink, or, in some way, disturbed the order of how the teacher wanted it to look. Then he innocently sat back down by the time the teacher opened the door. Any resistance on my part just made the mess worse.

Needless to say, I was the one who received a blow of the ruler on my open palm and there was nothing I could do about it. At least that is how I perceived it.

When I remembered this story, or told it to illustrate either bullying, or the harsh discipline first grade boys were exposed to in post-war Hungary, I did not think (or believe) that this incident had any other influence upon me or in my life.

My Story

Part 2: How I Formed, Played Out and Resolved One Childhood Belief

Thirty years later, when I married, I would not allow my wife to touch my desk. It was the messiest part of our entire household. We used to joke about it and make excuses to friends and visitors. I claimed that as a writer I kept producing publishable material, and that the chaos was the well from which the creative material formed!

It was a clever but an empty rationalization!

Three decades later, on a holiday to a Central American Pacific beach, a friend burst into my room while I was writing. I had my door partially open for the fresh sea air. He asked me a question. We had a short discussion. We were both satisfied and he turned to leave.

Somewhat obsessive/compulsive, he kept playing with the door on his way out. He said he could not hold the door open at the angle at which he found it. The door kept closing as he let go. So he reached over to my desk, took an empty water bottle and placed it on the floor. It didn't hold the door. Then he took a full water bottle, and that held! But as I watched him take things off my desk, a sudden rage arose in my belly and I bellowed at him with a full-chested roar to keep his hands off my desk and get out of my room!

I was totally surprised at myself. In turn, my friend was totally surprised at me. In thirty-five years of friendship he had never heard me lose my temper! He scurried off, out of range of my anger. He had no idea what he had done 'wrong'.

Suddenly, a moment after my outburst, I began to laugh. My friend came back, looked in and asked, "Are you laughing at me?"

"No," I said, "I am laughing at myself. Now go. I will tell you later. I must write this one down."

What happened was that even as I was yelling, I began to see my friend as the first-grade bully who caused me so much pain in childhood.

At that point in my life, I had already begun a year-long study and practice for a Compassionate Inquiry certification course. I was already open to the possibility that some of my words and actions would be unconscious reactions to beliefs and unresolved emotional trauma.

I had forgotten my first-grade story, and I had repressed those repeated humiliations in front of my peers. In that Nicaraguan motel room, however, I made the connection between that series of early classroom incidents and my jealous guarding of the sanctity of my desk space.

I had developed an unconscious belief that I would be punished if someone messed with my desk.

Puff! The belief disappeared. After that, I began to let anyone have their way with my desk: cleaners, writer friends, girlfriends, (I was divorced already), as long as they did not shuffle my papers.

Jealously guarding the sanctity of my desk because of an unconscious fear of punishment was a belief for which, I was not responsible either as a child, or as an adult.

What is the Boundary Between Illusions and Delusions?

This is a trick question, of course! The Buddha said that all our perceptions are illusions. When our insecurities magnify our illusions to impractical levels, we enter the realm of delusions.

Am I responsible for my illusions and delusions? It is a choice. I can live unawares and not worry that most everything I believe is an illusion. My perceived reality, then, is technically an illusion. Similarly, those wishes that cannot be realized are all delusions. Nobody will stop me from my illusions and delusions unless I break some laws, rules, or regulations. Nobody will stop me unless my illusions or delusions interfere with someone else's peace of mind.

It is my relationship with people around me that defines my illusions and sets the boundaries for my delusions. If I have a family and believe that since I bring home the money, their sole purpose is to serve me, I would be in serious, delusional trouble.

If I believed that sexual relationships serve only the short-term goal of bringing me pleasure, I would be in serious, delusional trouble! Rightly or wrongly, I believe that, although privilege exists, taking it for granted, or believing that I deserve it, is the beginning of delusion.

Perception

Part 1: Illusion or Reality?

Thoughtful Quantum Physicists have theorized for over a century that matter turns into energy, and back to matter something like 10^{52} times per second That's fast. Considering that an old film reel had to run at a speed of 24 frames per second for me to reach the illusion that I am seeing something continuous, the Quantum speed of change between matter and energy wins, hands down.

The trick to my illusion is that I am burdened by my senses and perceptions. These burdens allow me to see only the physical half of actuality. Because I interpret ALL of my feelings and judgments via my senses and perceptions, I am unable to perceive or connect with my body as energy. I am unable to perceive or connect with energy outside of me, except through objects or instruments. I can, however, feel good in certain environments. For example, I was once 'caught' in Lincoln Cathedral in England, absent-mindedly walking and gazing at the marvelous gothic arches above me. A young Church Army student asked me if I was lost.

Without thinking I said, "I am looking at a thousand years of prayer that had accumulated under those arches." The student slowly backed away from me. What I said, in effect, acknowledged in unrehearsed poetic words the possibility that I was seeing or experiencing energy. Perhaps the energy of prayer. We can confidently claim to have 'harnessed' electricity, electromagnetism, radio waves, nuclear and other radiation and lots of other energy states, but we have not harnessed, nor understood, much less used in a consistent and beneficial way, the energy of love.

This is probably because we seek it outside of ourselves.

Perception

Part 2: Is Illusion My Reality?

Yes.

Perception

Part 3: Who Do I Think I Am?

I was kidding!

The greatest arguments against illusion being our reality are danger and technology.

The argument for danger goes like this:

If I put my finger into the fire, my finger will be burnt. The resulting pain, reddening of the skin, and possible third-degree-burn signs make the entire experience 'real', and not illusory.

The counter-argument to this experience is fire-walking.

Let's look at the facts. I have a very highly trained intellect. I went through 21 years of formal education between Grade 1 and abandoning a PhD. My intellect was constantly challenged, and I had to change, learn, adapt, and become creative.

This was never more so than when I was preparing for a fire walk! But there is more to my 'training' in spirituality and intuition.

I had spent fifty years in formal spiritual studies via fundamentalist Christianity, Zen Buddhism, The Rosicrucians, Anthroposophy, Jungian Dream Analysis, and on and on. These studies constantly challenged me to slow down my 'mind' (not the intellect), slow down and deepen my breathing, calm my body and tap into the infinite possibilities that comprise the universe. The net result of all these studies is a trust in inner guidance, as if from a divine (universal) source. The litmus test is simple: what I think, say and do has to be beneficial for me, for those around me, and for the entire planet.

Does it work? NO!

(Well, sometimes.)

What keeps me from consistently reaching my three benefits? It has nothing to do with illusion and delusion.

What keeps me from consistently reaching my three benefits is childhood trauma, and a hidden set of repressed emotions that I have unconsciously carried all my life. It is a deep emotional disconnect with which I unknowingly sabotage my life at every level. There are coping mechanisms, but I want *healing*.

Add to this intellectual and intuition-trusting training, a lifetime of physical exercise and healthy eating/drinking, and I should be living the pure life guided by the intelligence of the heart, the only intelligence I acknowledge.

The joy of being human, however, is that I have liberally partaken of distractions, closed my eyes and ears time and again to the calling of my intuition and heart-centered guidance, and got myself overweight and quite ill at times, all in the name of exercising my freedom of choice.

Another way of saying it is that I freely indulged in my illusions!

Perception

Part 4: Fire Walking: An Object Lesson to Recognize Illusion

With my solid background in all these studies on spirituality and intuition, I went to a fire-walking event in Allegan, Michigan some years ago. We built the wood pile under the supervision of a trained fire-builder, then spent two hours being indoctrinated, and two more hours walking around in a circle, repeating the mantra, "I feel cool, soft, velvety grass under my feet; I feel cool, soft, velvety grass under my feet …"

When the coals were red hot and raked into an even surface, we were ready to 'walk' through the five or six steps it took to cross the burning square.

I was mortally scared. My intellect told me that I was going to be burned. There was no alternative in my mind. I watched other people cross the coal-garden, and I marveled at them smiling in triumph. Then, a gentle man in his eighties grabbed my hand and said, "Daniel, let's cross together!"

My instinct was to draw my hand right back out of his grasp, but he was like a teacher to me, and I didn't want to disobey his wishes. After all, I had seen him cross the fire-garden twice already, so I knew that he did not mean any harm. So I went, thinking I would get burned, the hosts would have to call an ambulance and I would be rushed to the emergency room. I would be treated for burns all over my feet, and the fire-walking ceremony would be shut down.

What the hell?!

Holding the old teacher's hand, I walked onto the hot coals and all I felt was cool, soft, velvety grass under my feet. I laughed insanely at the other end, and wondered at the powerlessness of my intellect—my script-running mind. Why did these not know that there is another reality? How did the fire-walking script supersede a lifetime of the belief that fire will burn me?

The old teacher grabbed my hand again, and once again we stepped into the fire-garden. Again, I fully believed, and thought to myself, that I was going to get burned and that the magic of the mantra had likely worn off. But, no. All I felt while walking on the "hot coals" was cool, soft, velvety grass under my feet.

Perception

Part 5: Technological Reality?

The argument against illusion from a technological point of view is this: Let's say, I discover the "sword-in-the-stone." I don't mean that I become Arthur, the young lad who innocently pulls the sword out of the stone and becomes the king of ancient England. I mean that I discover iron ore, and find a way of extracting the iron through heating the ore, and with the resulting iron I hammer out a sword. "Sword-in-the-Stone" was the ancient code word for iron ore, recognized only by initiated iron smelters. Eventually, it was used as propaganda to have everyone accept Arthur as their king.

Is that sword made of iron ore real or an illusion? If I run that sword through someone who attacks me, that attacker will die. The apparent cause and effect are real in the sense that they are predictable and repeatable.

Our entire technological world is based on this predictability and repeatability. As long as something is predictable and repeatable, it is not an illusion. So goes the technological argument.

This process, which works for matter, was then applied to human beings through propaganda. It was called religion and government.

In the ancient world, there were two outstanding 'deities' who taught their people agriculture, government and religion. One was Osiris to the people in northeast Africa. The other was Viracocha to the people in South America ruled by the Incas.

Teach the people to believe in something (and it doesn't make any difference what that 'something' is) and they become predictable and will repeat the same daily/weekly/monthly/annual cycles as long as they live.

In my time, entire disciplines dedicated to the study of my habituated tendencies have come into being: sociology, psychology, demographics, and, more recently, we have Google and Facebook where every click becomes a predictor as to what I am likely to respond to, and therefore, what I am likely to buy.

My brainwashed, habituated, predictable and repeatable way of life is real, and not an illusion. I can be certain of that, because anything that can be measured is real, right?

It is more likely that measurement (any kind of quantifying) is a way to manage my illusions!

Are there other realities outside our illusions?

Who Speaks Through me?
Am I Responsible?

Some time ago, I was dating a lovely, highly educated woman. She appealed to me in every way, and it seemed as if I appealed to her as well. It looked like it could be a workable relationship.

I asked if I could spend the night with her, and she smiled and accepted. As the evening wore on, she began to drink wine—four, or five glasses, and finally she said, "I am ready!"

As it happened, I was quite unaware at the time, and I thought 'I had gotten lucky.' I also thought that I was rather intelligent AND sensitive, until a 'mentor' came along and said that alcohol, drugs, and hallucinogens put people into a trance state where the 'spirit' of that substance takes over the consciousness.

After four or five glasses of wine (nearly a bottle) it was the alcohol that was speaking through my partner. Yes, I was making love to her body, but my communication was with the spirit of the alcohol!

Sure, there are extenuating circumstances, and many ways to rationalize my partner's dependence on alcohol to accept the sexuality that her body 'wants' or 'needs', but her mind—her belief system—forbids.

As it was, she came from an Evangelical upbringing where sex before marriage was strictly forbidden. I really should say 'discouraged', because very few of the young men and women actually kept themselves celibate until they married.

The current culture gives mixed messages. Language is ambiguous, and the bottom line is that I have to make a choice as to how I am going to behave and act. Which means that I am the one who is ultimately responsible.

I often attempt to give up this totally natural sense of responsibility. Instead, I adopt a 'situational ethic'. That is, "I will know what to do (I will make a choice) when the time comes!"

I am still the one who makes that situational choice. There is no way out of being responsible except through unconsciousness. As a result, when life becomes difficult, I opt for unconsciousness.

My Story

Part 1: The Facts About One Relationship

I fall asleep after two glasses of wine. I resent the intrusion of TCP (from marijuana) into my consciousness. For some reason I prefer a walk through the woods, to watch a waterfall, or see flames reaching up from a bonfire to a mind-altering substance. I would rather hear ocean waves crashing against the rocks., or listen to some beautiful music.

But that's just me.

Each to his own.

For the short time we were together, my partner and I remained unaware of our inner struggles. Our repressed fears guided our conversations and we did not know it. Drinking just a bit too much alcohol was my partner's way of soothing her pain. Hiding in my room, obsessively writing was my way of soothing mine.

How did we communicate?

First of all, neither of us had to 'soothe our pain' all of the time. We often reached an unselfconscious space. It was a space and a time where we both felt unconstrained by the belief systems of our upbringing. We laughed and talked (about other things, never about ourselves) freely, walked the wild trails and bicycled, entertained and went to shows and concerts with not a thought of inner trauma.

When we reached home and still had energy for a cuddle, all was well. But when that turned into passion, out came the bottle. When I wanted to talk about 'it' in the morning, "I don't want to talk about it," was the answer. I retreated into my study and wrote letters, articles, essays, journals, and poems—all left unpublished. We ended the relationship amicably, but in my mind, I had left being in a trance.

My Story

Part 2: Analysis of the Fear That Speaks Through Me

What were all those writings about? Now that I can look back with hindsight, they were my fears. But I did not know that. I was not afraid of my partner. I accepted her decision not to talk about our relationship. I was afraid of hurting her.

The few times we actually reached a conversation, we disagreed, and my voice grew louder. I probably believed that if I raised my voice she would hear me. I was frustrated at not being heard. I may have raised my voice because both my mother and father raised their voices if I didn't do what they told me. I seemed to have forgotten that their raised voice did not result in me doing what they wanted! Their raised voice just rammed my repressed fears even deeper. When these deep-set fears began to speak through me, I did not recognize their source.

I projected these fears, unknowingly, onto my partner.

Who Speaks to Me?

My garden and lawn have been invaded by an army of dandelions. My first reaction was to go to the hardware store and buy a weed killer. My conscience, however, told me that if I use it, I will poison my entire lawn and I won't be able to walk barefoot over my own property.

My 'reaction' then shifted to a more thoughtful 'response'. What were my options?

I could dig each and every dandelion out of the earth. That seemed like a lot of work. OK. I decided not to dig them up. My next choice: I would start picking dandelion leaves and I would eat them. That one worked. It was healthy.

I took a weekend course with the Dandelion Doctor, a herbalist from Detroit. He taught us that dandelions contained 64 of the 67 known nutrients at the time. Today, there are 300 nutrients listed in the Merck Manual, but iceberg lettuce only contains 13 of these!

Now the dandelions speak to me. We have come to a live-and-let-live agreement, in a kind of a win-win situation. In the process, my perspective on the lawn and the gardens has changed. Dandelions are now OK. I eat them! I eat them with love and respect.

It is as if the entire lawn speaks to me, grateful that I did not use herbicides. I find this perspective viable.

Do I Perform Ceremony? Who is Responsible for It?

I have hundreds of unconscious habits that I repeat day in and day out. Because they are unconscious, they don't elevate me. They are routine. I take them for granted. One problem is that these habits don't necessarily serve me. Yet, in every sense of the word, all my habits qualify as rituals. I have no idea I perform them day in and day out.

These 'rituals' include the morning toilet and the morning commune, if you are into that. Each carry many ritualistic repetitions.

Communal ceremonies are not usually habitual, or routine events, but are nevertheless rituals. These might include a church service, a school graduation ceremony, a citizenship-granting court, or taking part in an aboriginal festival. Public ceremonies are usually enacted with full consciousness. I am there because I want to be.

The experience of children at these kinds of rituals of course, might be an exception. If I take my children to church because I believe it's "good for them" and they sit there totally self-consciously wondering what other people think of them, what secrets they hide from them, and what dirt they know about each, the ceremonial aspect of the service will go right over their heads. They may easily miss the communal delight of whatever is being celebrated.

Reaching back into the past, let me appeal to the Hermetic rule of balance—As Above, So Below, or As Outside, So Inside. In my interpretation, it is necessary to supplement and balance the outer ceremonies and celebrations with inner ones.

How to do that? The best way is to devise one from scratch. I can say that now, but the fact is I didn't begin that way! I borrowed a ceremony from The Rosicrucians. I took a glass of water and celebrated it as the universal solvent, as 70-80 percent of my body, as one of the four elements, and so on. I 'filled' my glass of water with love and light. I 'filled' it with the Vital Life Forces of the Universe. I held it to my solar plexus, pulsated it with energy, then drank every drop of it so it would transfer all its vitality into my being.

I still perform this ceremony once a day. It is the very first thing I do each morning after my toilet rituals.

Drinking this glass of water is not a responsibility. It is a consciously chosen discipline to celebrate my being, my life, my failures, and my accomplishments. If I didn't celebrate, if I didn't make up other ceremonies and rituals, the alternative would be to keep busy mindlessly in order to fight boredom, or descend into depression. The resulting negative state of mind would attract real or imagined illnesses. But these 'alternatives' are 'woulds' and 'shoulds', which are delusions piled on illusions.

There is really no substitute for a good personal ritual.

Am I a Bully? Then I was Bullied Myself!

Let's say I enjoy learning as much as possible about other people's personal information. That makes me an information junky. However, if I use that information against you and take advantage of you, then I am a bully.

Are you going to let me bully you?

That depends. If you are a four year old—yes. Even as a teenager you might. But as an adult, you will only let me bully you

1) If I am your boss and you can't get another job and there is no ombudsman/woman to whom you can complain.
2) If you were bullied by your parents or at school as a small child and retain a belief of helplessness.
3) If you remain so unaware of your emotional state that you would rather be bullied than face the pain of exploring your own repressed emotions, which would release much of your pain and suffering.

The underlying belief that motivates bullying is powerlessness. "My parents (older siblings, school mates) bullied me when I was a child. Never again. They taught me well. This time I will be the tough guy!"

It is generally accepted that the government acts like a 'bully' and many people find themselves disempowered. Acceptance is an effective coping mechanism, but becoming politically active is even better.

In a book called *The Rebel Sell,* the authors cleverly prove that if I rebel against whatever disenfranchisement I believe oppresses me, that pure rebel creativity becomes the next fad or fashion.

Society and culture can also be considered as 'bullies'. Social pressures, especially on our behavior, and cultural pressure, such as being politically correct or 'believing' in climate change, are strong forces.

Writing this book may be an act of rebellion on my part in the world of mental health and addiction.

What is Emotional Pain?

According to psychotherapists, emotional pain is the last thing people want to talk about. Not being a professional, licensed psychotherapist, all I can do is walk circles around my own emotional pain and describe what I feel.

In one of my stories, above, my grandmother betrayed me. It was not the spanking that hurt. I don't remember that, and the physical pain would have passed rather quickly. But there was another hurt. In one sense, it was the loss of connection to my grandmother. I could no longer trust her. In another sense, it was the loss of connection to myself.

One of the most important developmental factors in a child's life is an ongoing relationship to his or her caregiver. Receiving love from my mother was good. But was she there for me? She didn't know she had to be 'there for me'! She had to go out and scrounge for food in a dangerous war situation. It wasn't her fault that she was not there for me as an infant.

In the case of my children, my wife had to work outside the home, and I was busy with my own work. We did not carry on a dialogue with our children in the same way our parents did not carry on one with us, except a few times a day. These dialogues with our children took place when they had to be fed or changed, or put to bed, or shown off to someone else. It was the lack of emotional contact that would have hurt them. It was the lack of emotional contact that would have hurt me in my childhood.

Let's look at emotional pain from another perspective. Children of alcoholic or drug-addicted parents mistake 'love' for the abuse they receive. Children simply don't know any better. All they need is loving contact—to be held. Instead, they are yelled at, beaten and otherwise abused. These children then mistake their abuse for love!

These children grow up, become hormone-driven young adults and guess who they marry? They marry abusive mates. Their true emotional potential did not develop, so they feel 'safe' when someone is angry at them. Anger and abuse are the only forms of contact they had as infants and toddlers.

Even a 'normal' childhood is a series of adaptations. Children adapt a behavior that will bring them closest to their parents/carers. As a child, I have to settle for the second best. I will smile, and I will coo, but it already covers up the pain of not actually being held in my mother's arms, or anywhere near her body.

That pain is suppressed, but somewhere, deep down, I feel hurt. The older I get, the more I deny it.

The more I deny the pain, the more it wants to come out.

How Do I Face my Emotional Pain?

Part 1: Who Will Help Me with How I Feel?

It would be funny (or sad) to count up all the times that I went to a medical doctor and he or she asked me, "How do you feel? Have you had any major emotional traumas or unusual stresses lately?"

My response: "None!"

Yet, all my doctors have been kind, and seemingly caring. They are trained to respond to symptoms. They are likely trained to respond to the parents of children, or to the "parent" in me. There is a good chance that some of our doctors are simply not interested in how we feel emotionally. Many believe it is not their role.

If I want to talk about my emotions, I have to go to a psychotherapist.

I was naive. I thought that since 'psyche' is the ancient Greek term for 'soul', a Psychotherapist would look into my soul. No. "Only priests do that," I was told. Then, I thought that perhaps, a psychotherapist could help me to look into my own soul. No. Psychotherapists can't even look into their own souls, much less help me take a look at mine. What the Fuck?

It turns out that no matter how enlightened the culture or civilization, very few people are ever asked to look into their own souls.

In fact, most of us so meticulously avoid being a voyeur into our own dramas, that we will go to great length to deny our own emotional pain. Most of us don't even have to deny it. We live so unconsciously, in such habituated lives that even if we keep making the same mistakes over and over again (like the children of alcoholics who keep marrying alcoholics) it never occurs to us that there is anything we can do about it. It never occurs to us that the repetitive problems we face, or the constant lashing out with which we can't help reacting to others, are the very signals our souls are sending out to have us look inside ourselves.

The bottom line is that we avoid facing our pain at any cost.

How Do I Face my Emotional Pain?

Part 2: How long have human being been aware of their pain?

The notion that human beings have emotional pain has been around for about two and a half millennia, for sure. That is about 2,500 years.

The Mahabharata, a sacred book of ancient India, purportedly goes back over 12,000 years and tells of epic wars. Wherever there is war, there is not just the physical pain that war causes, but it is usually emotional pain that causes the war in the first place.

Take a scene from the Bhagavad Gita, another Hindu sacred text, where Arjuna, the King, has a conversation with his personal deity, Lord Krishna. Arjuna is obviously upset over a brewing rebellion against him. He tries to argue with Lord Krishna by saying that he loves his Tutor, his brothers, and all the other people of the palace who have rebelled against him, and that it would pain him to harm them. Lord Krishna, however, would have none of that emotional stuff! He tells Arjuna that he was born a warrior and that his life's purpose is to fight and kill, if he has to.

Lord Krishna reminds Arjuna that he did not cause the rebellion himself. The rebels made a clear choice on their own, therefore, they will accept the consequences if the rebellion was to fail. Lord Krishna ends his speech to King Arjuna with these words (paraphrased): "'Just because you kill a man's body, do you think you can also kill his soul? Go, do the work you were born to do!'"

Buddhism developed around two and a half millennia ago. The Buddha's route to enlightenment was to go through all human experience. Among these, he felt emotional pain. He felt fear. Demons attacked him because of his fears. The Buddha worked through his options. He could either be emotionally destroyed by demons, or overcome his fears and face his pain. He overcame his fears. The demons disappeared because they had nothing to work with.

What does the Buddha's enlightenment mean? He was asked, "Are you God?"

The Buddha answered, "No! I am awake."

Seven hundred years later, a Tibetan monk wrote the text of the Tibetan Book of the Dead. He concealed the book, thinking the world was not ready for it. It did not hit the streets until the 14th century. Those lucky people who got a copy (mostly other Buddhist monks and Lamas) either already knew the message, or reading it opened their eyes. When the Tibetan Book of the Dead was finally translated into European languages, in the 20th century, about a hundred years ago, people took note. Carl Gustav Jung, the Swiss Psychiatrist, worked it into his comprehension of the human psyche. Why?

One of the most profound sayings or teaching in that book of treasure is this:

"Face your pain. If you don't face it, it will become worse!" The Tibetan Book of the Dead was talking about emotional pain.

How do I Face my Emotional Pain?

Part 3: Do I Have Any?

Our current psychiatric and neurobiological wisdom, consisting of mostly scientific studies accepts that most people experience childhood trauma. Every authority may differ on how to handle that trauma, but we can be certain that we have it!

From where do we get—or contract—childhood trauma?

It is simple and astounding at the same time! When you and I were fetuses in our mothers' womb, there were likely only two emotions available to us: wellbeing and discomfort. Neither our mother nor our father had any say whether or not we felt one or the other. It is not that they didn't love me, or you! Our developing being was subject to forces beyond their control.

What were those forces? Our feelings, as fetuses, were entirely determined by our mothers' hormonal system!

Mothers, of course, have very little (if any) control over their hormonal systems. If she was having a good day, or if someone was nice to my mother, she felt good. Her body produced all the 'feel-good' hormones like serotonin and oxytocin. As her unborn child, I contentedly bathed in her amniotic fluid, within those 'feel-good' surroundings. But then, a mouse scurried across the floor, or an angry landlord threatened to evict the family, or an unexpected death in the family happened. The list of what can cause a pregnant mother stress goes on and on and includes alcohol and drugs, violence and shame. Whatever it was that stressed her, in response, my mother began to produce adrenaline and cortisol—her own survival hormones.

When the amniotic fluid was filled with adrenaline and cortisol, matters changed for me. I was helplessly floating in my mothers' belly when her survival hormones shut me down! It is not just that, as a fetus, I became very unhappy and very uncomfortable. Researchers say that the loss of my mothers' feel-good hormones became a survival issue for me. The survival instinct is the only defense mechanism available to fetuses and infants!

In the late nineteen seventies, researchers already knew that my mother's survival hormones actually stopped my development as a fetus.

At whatever stage of my development I was when this occurred, I became constricted. I waited, as a developing fetus in my mother's belly for the adrenalin and cortisol to be washed out of my mother's blood stream, and for it to be replaced by serotonin and oxytocin. Only when I felt comfortable again did my physical development continue. But, that development continued not where it left off, but where it would have been after that elapsed time. It left parts of me undeveloped or only partially developed, as a fetus. This process of uncomfortably constricting as a fetus and shutting down growth has emotional consequences! There is even the possibility that the fetus experiences pain every time the mother's survival hormones kick in. More studies are needed to show what many experts suspect, that when the mother's survival hormones are finally replaced with her 'feel-good' hormones, although the physical development resumes, the emotional development does not!

It is not the mother's fault. She is not responsible for her unexpected stresses.

CHAPTER

36

How do I Face My Emotional Pain?

Part 4: What is Trauma?

Whatever a fetus can do to bring back oxytocin and serotonin, I likely tried it. In the process of continued loss and return of these 'feel-good' hormones, however, I was traumatized! Trauma, Dr. Gabor Maté explains, is not the experience of a stressful situation; it is the internal response to it. Trauma is the separation from our own emotional self. In turn, Dr. Maté refers to his own teacher, A.H. Almaas, who said, "The fundamental thing that happened, and the greatest calamity, is not that there was no love or support. The greater calamity that was caused by that first calamity (such as the loss of oxytocin) is that you lost the connection to your essence. That loss of connection is much more important than whether your father or mother loved you or not." The loss of connection to one's authentic self is much more important than what happened.

It's not about the fact that as a fetus, I didn't know what was happening. Of course I didn't. I was at a stage of my life where feeling good meant I remained alive. Feeling uncomfortable meant that I might die. Even as an unformed human being, I had my survival instincts awakened by these changes in my mother's bloodstream.

I didn't even know what pain was, yet I already had experienced it. And with that first experience of pain, I began to create responses that would bring back homeostasis.

As an adult, I find it curious that as a fetal human organism I was already working on something that was available, but not in my power to control. I had to focus on bringing back the good feelings. I had lost my ability to remain connected with those good feelings, which should have formed my authentic emotional self.

How Do I Face My Emotional Pain?

Part 5: What About the Pain of Birth?

Is birth painful? Just look at the very first book of the Old Testament (or the Torah) and you will find that God had cursed humankind right from the start by commanding all women to birth their children in pain. Most women just take that curse and believe it, apply it, perform it, accept it and live with it. But I have spoken with friends who claimed that: "When I was pregnant, I took long walks, ate lots and lots of ice cream, and when the time came, the kid just popped out and I was on my feet again as good as new. It was painless"

OK, that is the exception to the rule. There are books and books about the pain of birth for the mother.

What about the child?

What about the psychological impact of birth on the child?

Just for fun, make a list of all the changes that occur all at once, as the fully formed child (or a premature one) comes through the 'birth canal' or is taken out through c-section. The newborn comes from heat into cold, from darkness into light, from the sounds of a mother's heartbeat to a cacophony of unfamiliar noise. There are likely many other contrasts.

I was pulled out with a pair of cold forceps. It must have been awkward and painful. My mother told me that the nurse picked me up and showed me to her. When she saw me, my mother burst into tears and thought, "What monster did I give birth to?" The forceps had disfigured my skull and made my face swell to twice its size. There was nothing cute about me. There certainly was physical pain. There also must have been an array of emotional shock and pain.

We don't associate newborn children with pain. We don't often think that newborns feel pain. Otherwise, why would doctors circumcise boys on the first few days of their lives? In his book, *The Magical Child*, Joseph Chilton Pearce noted in a study (1977) that newborn boys who were not circumcised smiled within the first four days of life. Circumcised boys began to smile only in their sixth week of life.

Being held by a mother, it seems, can overcome the trauma of birth, therefore it should also overcome the trauma of circumcision. Certainly, the physical pain subsides in a day or three. But the emotional trauma of adding insult to injury (the trauma of circumcision after the trauma of birth) lasts a long time. For whatever reason, newborn children and circumcised boys are often separated from their mothers.

As it turns out, such traumas in infancy and in early childhood last a lifetime. Every one of us carries the pain of our childhood into our adulthood.

How come we don't know it? Because that pain was usually pre-verbal. We could not put our complaint into words. It remained a feeling. It remained an unnamed pain. As far as human beings are concerned, if something doesn't have a name and cannot be measured, such as fetal trauma or the pain of birth for the child, it doesn't exist.

Right!

CHAPTER

38

Becoming Aware

Part 1: Why Habits and Thoughtlessness Get in the Way

Philosophers, neuroscientists and psychologists continue to debate the question, 'What is 'consciousness?''. While it may be true that we need consciousness to be, or to become aware, the process of becoming aware takes place in this endless quagmire of undefined psyche.

For example, Jung's theory of 'individuation' is a well-debated process. Individuation changes our consciousness. But most people go through the process of individuation unconsciously!

Every teenager goes through a phase of intense self-consciousness. I used to believe that everyone watched me, and I played to my imagined audience. Most people, however, never leave that phase and remain self-conscious, (though not self-aware) throughout their lives.

What is awareness? What is 'self-awareness'? What did the Buddha mean when he said, "I am awake?"

It comes down to this: I can do something habitually, and, because I am doing it by rote, even though I may be 'aware' that I am pushing my children out of the way so that I can finish watching the ballgame, I am unconscious of the consequences of what I am doing. There is a game-changing example that, at least in the Christian communities of the world, points to this dissociation between local awareness and general unconsciousness. Each Easter, when Christians re-read or even re-enact the crucifiction, burial and resurrection of Jesus, they read Jesus' words from the cross: "Forgive them, Father, for they know not what they do!"

Habitual behavior is akin to addiction. I have a localized thought, or something I say, or do (or all three) and I pass on to the next 'thing' without seeing the larger picture.

I don't ask how I feel about what I just thought, said, or did. I simply don't know what I am doing, neither know nor care what I have done. Jesus on the cross could just as well have said those words to me!

Childhood trauma is generational. It has been passed down from parents to their children for millennia. We know not what we are doing when we fail to hold our children with love and compassion. We exhibit cultural ignorance when we cannot teach children to cope and get over trauma.

In contrast, there are times when I am very aware of what I am doing. For instance, I am very aware when I am drinking a cold glass of beer, or soda pop. When the cool, sparkling liquid flows down my throat, I definitely stop and feel it. I may even respond to it with a satisfied sigh, a word of praise, or just a happy belch.

What does it take to be emotionally connected to, or aware of more of my thoughts, words and deeds?

Becoming Aware

Part 2: How Do I Find a Therapy or Therapist?

OK, don't panic, there are millions of different ways of becoming aware. That is part of the problem. When an anxious child is given a dozen different toys to choose from, his or her anxiety levels go up. When a traumatized, emotionally repressed adult is given a thousand different ways of becoming aware, that vast choice will simply heighten the already existing inner stress.

It might now be useful to note a growing disconnect with the current practice of Psychiatry. Year after year, new psychiatric disorders are added to an already very long list of our problems. The list may be growing due to the fact that Psychiatrists work with drugs and there is pressure from the pharmaceutical industry to create more drugs—and thus, prescribe more. The use of pharmaceuticals is beside the point, though. The disconnect is that there is only one underlying problem that may prove to be the cause of all psychiatric conditions as well as most diseases! And that problem is that we have become disconnected from our potential emotional selves. In other words, not only are the multitudes of psychiatric disorders just variations of one basic trauma as pointed out in the Introduction, Part 1, but also that that trauma can now, for the first time in our history, can be managed by facing, accepting and releasing that repressed, bottled-up pain.

In order to begin the process of reconnection, it's best to begin with one therapy. The beautiful part of beginning to become aware is that if it is not the 'right' therapy (or therapist) for you, you can leave or fire the therapist (nothing personal, right?), and start with another one.

There are, of course potential pitfalls. Some therapies cost an arm and a leg. For example, when I was finally ready to enter a program that I felt would guide me into my own self-awareness, mindfulness and towards self-compassion, the one I chose cost $1600.00 Canadian Dollars (about $1200.00 US).

That cost seemed too high for a first try. There were hundreds of other therapies available, but I did not know about them. Even when people mentioned some of the others, I would not listen. It was only when someone told me that Dr. Gabor Maté was coming to town (Owen Sound, Ontario, Canada) that something resonated with me that what he had to say, or teach might be the right therapy for me.

At first, I just shrugged my shoulders and dismissed the thought. This man was an addiction specialist and I did not consider myself an 'addict'. But a friend repeated the news, and told me about the two books Dr. Maté had written. One of them attracted me very strongly. It is called *In the Realm of Hungry Ghosts*. The other book is *When the Body Says No!*

The closer the date came for his workshop, the more certain I became that this man "spoke my language." He did, in two different ways. First, he was Hungarian, as am I, and we were born within two months of each other, just as the German army occupied Hungary. Such coincidences— one could even call them synchronicities—are incidental, but Dr. Maté also "spoke my language" in the sense that he was able to present scientific research about trauma on the one hand, and illustrate that research with traditional wisdom-teachings on the other. In my eyes, his left-brain logical mind was well balanced with right-brain creativity.

I signed up for that workshop before I committed myself to a therapy, and I have never looked back. Dr. Maté also influenced the Beyond Addiction Program-the Yogic Way of Recovery that Sat Dharam Kaur, ND developed and teaches around the world. I was fortunate, or perhaps soul-guided, to find the right therapy for myself on my very first exploration.

CHAPTER

40

Becoming Aware

Part 3: What's the First Step to Finding a Therapist?

Let's say that I complain of having "dark thoughts". "Dark thoughts" can range from being disappointed with myself, or not believing I am worthy of other people's love, to feelings of total uselessness and even suicide. A dark thought is usually cyclical and keeps coming back at the most inconvenient times.

Whatever it is that darkens my world sneaks upon me again and again. It is a continuous thought process with which I have dug myself into darkness for years, perhaps decades.

Next, I have to imagine that the first episode of this 'darkness' was likely a childhood trauma that became exaggerated year by year, decade by decade, and each time it got worse, I had only limited ways to soothe it:

1. With substances (whatever these may have been, it doesn't matter). But the temporary soothing did not heal the darkness.

2. Through repression. But repressing feelings, making myself unconscious of my own feelings, made me ill and started chronic problems that lasted for years.

3. By telling someone about my dark thoughts. The very act of making that contact and telling the listener that these 'dark thoughts' plague me is a positive, aware and self-caring act on my part.

If I am afraid of telling anyone, or am ashamed, then I condemn myself to more of this cyclical suffering. Being trapped in such a cycle continues until I find the courage, or the desperate need within myself to be heard.

Admittedly, I need a safe place and a safe listener who will not take advantage of me, or make fun of me. Family members may not be the best choice, unless I am still in my teens and have a mother or father, aunt or uncle, who might listen and/or help me find a caring professional.

Our world is beginning to be filled with caring, mindful, even compassionate professional therapists precisely because the need to release repressed emotions is starting to be seen as a solution to a multitude of social problems. Among such caring professionals are a growing number of certified Compassionate Inquiry practitioners. They can be found at http://compassionateinquiry.com/practitioners/

My best option is to get over my fears and lack of trust, and ask to see a professional therapist.

Becoming Aware

Part 4: How Do I Search for My Repressed Feelings?

Here is an exercise you might do at any time, at your convenience. Think of someone from your childhood, or later in your life who has deeply hurt you.

If that someone has died, ask yourself how you would mourn him/her if s/he was your closest and most beloved friend/partner in the whole world. You might yell in despair, cry, reason-out why you lost him/her. As you go through this exercise, be aware of your body sensations and note what feelings come up. If you are not clear which are feelings/emotions and which are perceptions and interpretations, Wikipedia has a handy list under the heading: Emotions.

However, if that person who hurt you so badly is still alive, imagine taking him/her out for dinner and celebrating him/her for being your most important teacher!! So many life coaches have adopted this solution, that Dr. Joe Dispenza suggests it in his books, CDs, and public lectures. He repeats this solution because it works!

How does it work?

By hurting me, someone has allowed me to get in touch with my feelings. Getting in touch with my feelings is the focus of this exercise.

Without a purpose or intent, dark thoughts sometimes come upon me. I picked up this exercise to change my perspective. It allow me to follow through with my healing intentions. I feel the pain this person has caused me, and feel thankful if I can, or just thank that person in my thoughts.

In a world where everyone is traumatized as children, which is my world as well as your world, each of us has a unique response to the pain we carry. Each of us has to come up with a unique solution to accept and cope with the effects of that trauma and absolve ourselves. Absolution includes myself as the child who was hurt, as well as whomever hurt me (my abuser). Further, I absolve my abuser and reverse any blame and resentment against him/her. At the end of the exercise, or at the end of a series of repetitions of the exercise, I can reassess who I am without carrying, and being played by that powerful trauma.

My Story: Another Boy Threw a Rock at My Head

Part 1-The Facts as I Remember Them

At the age of five, my grandmother came to our apartment to look after me for the day. At that point she had already betrayed me (see the first My Story, above), but she was useful in 'protecting' me in public. At least, that is what I heard from my parents.

She often walked me to the local park, St. Stephen's Park along the Danube River, right across from Margaret Island with all its swimming pools, sports facilities and spas. St. Stephens was "my" park. It had a pool-sized oval sand area 35 feet long and a bit more than 15 feet wide. The sand was at least 2 1/2 feet deep. I could build mountains and castles, as well as deep valleys, or make a marble path 8-10 feet long! I loved that sand-pit.

On one particular visit, there was only one other boy, approximately my age, who was also playing in the same sand-pit. We each played by ourselves. He, too, was accompanied by his grandmother, but our two guardians did not speak to each other. My grandmother was not from my own neighborhood.

The other grandmother 'directed' her grandson, and kept managing him and controlling him. Mine left me alone. The other boy soon tired of his 'play' and they left.

Sometime later, perhaps at lunch-time, my grandmother told me we must leave. I may have protested, but I remember that she had to take my hand and pull me after her.

The park also had manicured, pebble-strewn paths with benches dotted along the way. I was surprised to see the other boy from the sandpit sitting on the pebbles and his grandmother sitting on the bench, in utter silence. As we passed, the boy and I looked at each other.

No sooner had I passed, when a fist-sized chunk of broken concrete hit me on the back of the head, causing me to black out momentarily. I yelled out in pain, and then began to pull my grandmother's arms to get her to stop and bring the culprit to justice. "What happened?" she asked me. Between sobs, I told her about being hit, blacking out, and now the hurting at the back of my head.

My grandmother looked at the back of my head. There was no bump. She looked at the other grandmother who shrugged her shoulders. The other boy played innocently with the small pebbles on the ground next to his grandmother. My grandmother also shrugged her shoulders, said something I don't remember and began to pull me home again. I looked back at the other boy with undisguised hatred!

CHAPTER

43

My Story

Part 2: What Happened Next—The Feelings, Interpretations, and The Consequent Beliefs

I was not aware of rivalry or competition at the time. If I participated in these seemingly perfectly natural childhood behaviors, I did it unconsciously.

As far as I can remember, I was looking at this boy totally innocently when I passed by him. It was a matter of recognition, but since there was no response from him, I did not wave, or make any signs of friendship.

The stone against my head came as a total surprise! Chances are I sucked in my breath and pulled so hard on my grandmother's arm that she stopped. I was angry! I saw, (or imagined) a smirk on the boy's face. I knew he did it on purpose, because he must have found and held that small chunk of concrete for a few moments while my grandmother and I approached him.

I had no idea of the odds that a five-year-old child's stealthy throw of a stone could hit me exactly between the two occipital bones, in the soft part of the skull. Technically, (which I did not know as a child) the occipital lobe behind those bones is the only place that the lobe is directly vulnerable. The chances that he would hit that exact spot were infinitely small, but the boy had his lucky day!

Beside the physical pain, the problem was my grandmother's lack of support. She did not see the stone, she did not see or hear the hit. Chances are, neither did the other grandmother. As the person who had been hit by a rock, I could not and would not believe that!

I was hit, I was in pain and I wanted acknowledgment. It didn't happen. I wanted justice. I wanted the other boy spanked. It didn't happen. My anger and disappointment at not having my expectation met, turned into the notion that "nobody cares" and my response was that "I am not being loved."

This process was totally unconscious! Nevertheless, these interpretations turned into lifelong beliefs about myself: if that boy was not punished, then he punished me for something I must have done in the sandpit. I was guilty, whether I had done anything wrong or not.

Another belief that I formed after this incident was that I was not heard, and I was not worth being bothered about. It is likely that I was totally unaware that my grandmother had already betrayed me once, less than a year before. I did not make any such connection. But I quickly quieted down and accepted the situation, even though I was seething with anger inside for hours. I even told my mother that evening when she came home. She, too, could not see any evidence of the rock hitting me. My mother neither acknowledged nor even seemed to care about what happened to me. I was not protected.

She had to make dinner.

Becoming Aware

Part 5: Find a Practice and Reap Happiness

It is not getting rid of the trauma that will bring me happiness. It is going through the exercise of reaching the pain that the trauma caused me in the first place that brings happiness.

No matter how much I talk with you, it will not bring you happiness. Yes, it can bring you temporary relief, because if I am a sensitive practitioner, you will be heard! But your pain, and my pain is hidden deep in our bodies, and in our psyches.

Since it is both somatic and emotional, how do I get in touch with the pain within me?

One way of accessing my inner pain is though daily exercise. Believe it or not, any exercise that will bring me into the discomfort of exposing my hidden fears and other emotions will bring me happiness.

Take Kundalini Yoga, for instance. If I do it to prove to myself that I can endure the discomfort of the long exercises, it is helpful to me, but not quite enough! I may not have touched my hidden feelings. But if I go inside my body and sense what I feel in whatever body part I am exercising, it is the beginning of self-awareness. When I do this, the feeling responds, comes out of hiding and makes me laugh or cry.

And that result produces happiness.

Am I Conscious?

Part 1: What Do I Know?

I believe I am, simply because I am alive. I am awake. Is there a relationship between being conscious or unconscious and awake or asleep?

If being conscious is being awake, it is a safe bet that when I am not asleep, I am conscious. However, being conscious or awake depends on being in the here-and-now. It depends upon being in the moment. When my mind is focused on what I have to do before 5:00 p.m. (17:00 for military and European readers) instead of what is happening for me in this very moment, then, technically, I am not in the moment and therefore, I am unconscious. Emotionally, I am asleep.

If I am daydreaming and at the steering wheel of a vehicle at the same time, what happens? I can pull a "Walter Mitty"—a hilarious short story of what can happen to a daydreamer. Most accidents occur when people are either worrying about what happened in the past, what plans they have for the future, or they are daydreaming.

When I worry about things I can do nothing about while I am on a journey, my autonomous nervous system takes over the driving. It is a well-trained survival function we each have, and it usually does a good job. If something unusual happens, like when a truck pulls out in front of me, it is a signal to return to the moment. My attention inevitably shifts back into the here-and-now. (And thankfully so!)

Am I Conscious?

Part 2: Who Shifts My Consciousness?

Who shifts my consciousness?
A poem by Daniel Kolos
I know there is a joystick, but …
is it the emotional impact
of the choices that do the shifting?
Perhaps my consciousness
is a helpless bystander.
Are will or intent
a part of my consciousness
or are they the choices?
Will my decision to "act
with discipline and do
yoga this morning," rise above
the emotional call
of a bacon and egg breakfast?
Who's in charge of the joystick?

Am I Conscious?

Part 3: Are Habits Unconscious?

"How you doin'?" is an often heard greeting. Its meaning is a basic acknowledgement from another that I am alive. However, as often as it is said, nothing more is said. No conversation follows this greeting.

Such a greeting is a habitual response to meeting people.

I was astounded to learn that I had habitual responses to people until I witnessed a friend build one. He was around fifty when he inherited a nice chunk of money. His daughter, a real estate broker, advised him to buy an investment house. He duly bought a very expensive house in a resort city. His plan was to rent it out for a month or two at a time to vacationers in the summer, and skiers in the winter.

As soon as the papers were signed with a two-month period to closing, my friend, who was socially very active, began to "tell his story." Every time he met someone, after the greeting he continued with, "Guess what? I just bought an investment house!" He would name the city and everyone immediately saw the potential. "No, I don't take possession for two months," became "No, I don't take possession for six weeks," or four weeks. The story grew to include the furniture his daughter had been collecting from trendy second-hand shops. "Can you imagine? I fell in love with this dining room set that she picked up for six hundred bucks. It would have cost me over two thousand!"

The more he told the story, the less he had to think about it. It rolled off his tongue, and I was fascinated because he didn't care who he told it to, he just launched into the story simply because it was there. Sometimes he would tell the same people the story a second time. He was totally pre-occupied with the task of becoming a landlord and the only thing he needed to remain conscious of was the time-span as the days to the completion of the sale approached.

Am I Conscious?

Part 4: Where is My Consciousness?

You may have noticed that I am not trying to answer the question, 'What is consciousness?' It is a debate that is ongoing, with experts writing books and articles, researching brain and neurological responses, even looking at cellular consciousness, and coming up with new thoughts and theories about it every day.

All I know is that I am conscious because I can feel my body's many sensations: my eyes becoming tired enough to bring on a headache, my feet sore from walking with shoes a bit too tight, a 'heavy' feeling in my stomach from a salmon steak eaten late into the night, a pleasurable sensation dancing body-to-body with someone I fancy.

The body knows a lot more than I give it credit for—a lot more than I pay attention to!

How much attention should I pay to my body?

All experience of the outside world takes place inside of me. Consciousness is inside of me. I may pay attention to what happens outside of me, but I experience it or am conscious of what is happening within me! I constantly judge, measure and interpret what I believe is outside of me, forgetting that all these judgments, measurements and interpretations are subjective, and based on how I feel at the moment. The more habituated these judgments, measurements and interpretations are, the less conscious I am of having separated myself from consciousness-in-the-moment.

Am I Alone?

Part 1: Introduction

The short answer is yes and no!

From which perspective can I approach this question?

First of all, whether I am alone or interpret my state as one of I 'feel' alone and abandoned, this notion has many, many variations. Physically and rationally, if I am in my house, apartment or room with walls, or even when there is distance between me and the nearest human being, I am physically alone. The bottom line, for me at least, is that I am alone in the sense that there is no one close enough to hug.

If I feel lethargic, sad or depressed, I could also 'feel' lonely. At the same time, if I 'feel' abandoned, I will have that 'feeling' even if I am in a crowd of happy revelers!

The shocking news is that 'feeling' "I am alone" is not a feeling. It is a perception. Among the many voices that teach and urge us to "get in touch with our feelings", I will quote one. Dr. Gabor Maté, in his Compassionate

Inquiry process, teaches practitioners to know this difference: feeling alone or lonely is a state of being based on a perception.

The state of abandonment is an adult belief system that obscures a repressed feeling. That is, "the adult's sense of abandonment is an implicit memory of a child's inner experience."

A person's identity may be tied up in the concept or interpretation of having been abandoned. The feeling, however, that a pre-verbal child most likely experiences, during a time of perceived abandonment is fear. It is most likely the fear of death. "If my mother leaves me, I will no longer have access to her milk and I will die!" The child, of course, does not reason these words out. The survival response to not seeing his or her mother automatically puts the child into fear and freeze mode.

A practitioner's role is to help the adult client move from the current belief of suffering from abandonment, to the actual problem of having been disconnected from their authentic self, and to do this without feeding words into the client's mind/mouth.

Compassionate Inquiry itself, is not a precise methodology, Dr. Maté insists, but a process fuelled and driven by the balanced use of the therapist's knowledge and intuition. Yet, "the approach aims at getting at the truth of a person's present experience and their sources in the past."

Am I Alone?

Part 2: Am I Disconnected?

On a strictly rational level, I can be alone, as I am writing this chapter. But am I disconnected?

As I look around me, I am surrounded by the familiar and comfortable 'things' of my study: Shelves of books, filing cabinets, an ergonomically comfortable chair and desk, two computers, paintings on the walls and a bowl of soaked walnuts and pecans if I want to snack absent-mindedly.

Do I have a connection to these 'things'? Not really. I have an acceptance of them. When I took a month-long writing retreat, house sitting for a friend, I felt just as comfortable in her house. Although I would like my environment to feel nurturing to me, I don't actually identify myself with my surroundings.

If I am 'connected' to a soft, stuffed leather chair, a silk rug on the floor and a million-dollar painting on the wall, and I identify with them, will those 'things' make me feel happy?

Since every human being has a 'heart' and a 'mind', and neuroscientists now talk about both functioning with the complexity of a brain. I have a choice of 'thinking' with one or the other—or both!

I have been trained rationally by spending twenty-one years of my life at school; eight years in elementary school, four years in high school, four at university, and five in graduate school. I may not be 'smart', but I know a damn lot. The bottom line is that I have learned to think rationally.

At the same time, I have studied in various spiritual and religious institutions, and philosophical organizations and I have practiced meditation for the better part of forty-eight years. Each study, each experience focused on my inner emotional awareness, on the development of my intuition, the 'divine' guiding voice within, and the connection to my 'eternal' Soul. None of this lifelong work was rational.

When I was seventy, I took a course called "Beyond Addiction-the Yogic Path to Recovery." I became aware that my lifelong self-harming habits were my addictions. These habits soothed me and kept the pain of my disconnection repressed. Early childhood (even fetal) trauma forced me to learn coping mechanisms so that I would survive. These coping mechanisms disconnected me from my potential emotional self, my authentic center.

Am I Alone?

Part 3: When Did it Start?

The neurobiological response to my survival being threatened was disconnection. My personal belief is that my childhood experiences of not having my needs met as an infant disconnected me from my "divine Soul." Dr. Maté prefers to call this disconnection "from one's authentic emotional development." The 'disconnection' part is science. Research shows that infants develop coping mechanisms to get their mothers' attention back when it has turned elsewhere. The "divine Soul" part is my choice of names for my emotions, or my limbic system—what I am aware of when I am in the moment.

How did I lose my mother's attention? How did I first become abandoned?

The simple and astounding answer is this: "When you and I were fetuses in our mothers' wombs." Right, I already went through the fetal cycle of being surrounded by oxytocin/serotonin one moment and adrenalin/cortisol the next. (See Chapter 34).

To recap, I, as a fetus (or you, as a fetus) felt comfortable and nurtured when my mother's bloodstream was filled with oxytocin/serotonin. But when my mother was stressed and her bloodstream filled with adrenalin/cortisol, I went into a life-and-death survival response. Even my cellular development stopped until these stress-hormones were 'washed' away and replaced.

Why? Because without oxytocin/serotonin I must have been uncomfortable. The only feelings available to me were contentment or fear of death. Without oxytocin/serotonin, I had no choice but to feel that I would die!

I was alone.

Am I Alone?

Part 4: What's My Perspective?

Almost everyone grows up to believe "I am alone." At the same time, every one of us has a need for connection or contact. My first 'contact' was my mother. Accordingly, throughout life, everyone seeks love and connection, one of the six basic human needs according to Tony Robbins. This love connection can be a caregiver for a child, and or an adult, a friend, a lover, or a companion. But that 'someone' can also be a crowd, a team, a fighting unit, a stadium-full of strangers, or a public bus with people getting on and off.

Poets cannot stop writing about how lonely they feel in crowds. So what's the problem?

As long as I believe that my entire world exists "out there," I will most likely continue to hold the perception that I am alone. There are all these people, but no one to connect to. It reminds me of that famous quote, "Water, water everywhere, / Nor any drop to drink, lines from "The Rime of the Ancient Mariner," by Samuel Taylor Coleridge.

The next surprise is that both Quantum Theory shows and spiritual beliefs claim that the world is actually within me. Karl Pribram, a prominent neuroscientist and author of *The Holographic Brain,* was the first to prove that our eyes are "holographic decoder instruments." What is 'out there', he said, are innumerable Quantum energy fields, onto which our brains project form.

While it is true that each and every one of us learns to decipher and interpret those holographic patterns somewhat similarly, our fears, insecurities, pain, prejudices, belief systems, preferences, etc., each place a wall between ourselves and others. When I choose my 'tribe', in a larger sense I jump into a box with my own preferred people and believe that I am better and safer than people in other boxes.

I don't even have to believe in the Buddhist concept that this world is an illusion. Quantum Physics has already posited that reality.

My perspective, then, is that there are people around me, so I am not alone. I have friends, allies, and a support system. However, when someone "falls through the crack," that perspective shatters.

What crack? It could be the *Crack in the Cosmic Egg,* the Joseph Chilton Pearce book from the 1970s that examined various belief systems around the world. He proved that all belief systems work! When I "fall through the crack" in my own society, that is, when I lose the support I thought I had, my belief system is shattered. Whoever falls through the crack is alone.

Am I Alone?

Part 5: I Am Never Alone!

Dr. Gabor Maté, the founder of the Compassionate Inquiry method, says that we are born with a set of 'emotional possibilities', but that our fetal and early childhood experiences of not having our needs met separate us from that true self. The development of that authentic emotional potential is delayed because, as a child, I give up my own authenticity in order to secure my other need, which is attachment. As it happens, I don't succeed. Attachment to my parents or caregivers, while it is a human need and a survival drive, does not succeed. I spend the rest of my life believing that I have been abandoned. My survival response is to find ways to cope with abandonment.

One way of coping, of course, is to soothe the pain through addiction. Another is to seek and find that emotional, authentic self through yoga, meditation or a therapy such as Compassionate Inquiry.

Bruce Lipton posited that the hundred trillion or more cells in our bodies are all individually conscious, and that they all willingly give the management of their survival to our total body awareness, or holistic consciousness. If that is the case, not only am I never alone, but I live with a hundred trillion or more supportive consciousnesses, all of whom want me to succeed.

In other words, according to Bruce Lipton, I already live in the collective consciousness of my own body. And I have not even examined the role of my Soul!

Am I Alone?

Part 6: The Etymology and Religious Roots

The word, "Soul", carries lots of baggage.

I happen to be a recycler, not just with my garbage, but also with my words and concepts—with my abstract 'garbage'.

The word, "Soul", has a rich, but short history. The Old Testament distinguishes between a "living soul" and an "animal soul". The "living soul" or 'nedibah' in Hebrew, occurs only once, in Job 30:15. More recent translations render it 'honor'. However, the "animal soul", 'nephesh' in Hebrew, occupies four full columns in Young's Analytical Concordance of the Bible (1924). References to 'nephesh' in the Book of Psalms occupy one full column of those four!

There is a third form of the word, meaning "breath", 'neshamah' in Hebrew, that also occurs only once in Isaiah 57:16. The New Testament word for Soul is the Greek 'psuch' or 'psyche'.

Historically, however, the soul as 'nephesh' was first used while the Hebrews were in exile in Babylon between 600 and 500 BC. By then, Persian and Hellenistic influences equated 'nephesh' with the Greek 'psyche'.

Am I Alone?

Part 7: The Soul: Psyche in Greek Mythology

The Greek character, Psyche, was born an ordinary woman who was extraordinarily beautiful. She turned men's eyes away from The Goddess of Love, Aphrodite. This Goddess became jealous of Psyche and ordered Eros to go and cause Psyche to fall in love with the most hideous looking men. However, it was Eros who fell in love with Psyche, and carried her off (with or without her permission, we don't know) into his underground palace.

Eros instructed Psyche never to look upon his face. Psyche's sisters, however, taunted Psyche that Eros likely was the most hideous looking man of them all, so Psyche, who could not resist the need to know, looked at him, and Eros immediately abandoned her. Eventually she found 'employment' with Aphrodite, who set several impossible tasks for Psyche, including going into the realm of Hades and returning.

Psyche was somehow able to perform all the tasks Aphrodite gave her. The Gods on Mount Olympus celebrated Psyche's achievements and threw a great party for her. Eros, who also attended the party, was reunited with Psyche and Zeus, the King of the Gods, ceremoniously married them.

How, then, does Psyche turn up as the foundation of Psychology?

Am I Alone?

Part 8: Historical Separation of Religious and Intellectual Knowledge

Our Judeo-Christian religious 'roots' go back even as far as pre-biblical ancient Egypt via the Hebrew people. At the same time, we have a very strong intellectual tradition that also goes back to ancient Egypt, via the Greek philosophical tradition. The keepers of the religious traditions recognized that the philosophical/intellectual traditions would find cans and cans of worms in the religious belief systems, so both traditions flourished, separately.

These separate religious and intellectual traditions, though, brought us two completely different concepts or meanings for the word, "Soul."

In religious terms, it is our Soul that survives us and is at risk of going to Hell or spends eternity bored to death by the right hand of God. I don't know who made up those beliefs, but even as a deeply spiritual individual I find either choice unacceptable.

The intellectual tradition has kept "Soul" by its Greek name, Psyche, and that Greek mortal-turned-Goddess has become the foundation of several practices: the discipline of Psychology, Psychiatry and psychotherapy.

Carl G. Jung changed "Soul" as a potential Archetype, to "Self".

Literature has also played a part in using and defining "Soul" with words like "soulful" or "soulless".

Our Egyptologists have also chosen to translate two ancient Egyptian words, 'ba' and 'ka' as "soul" and "spirit". The 'ba' leaves the body in the tomb and is shown flying away. We don't know where it flies to, but it returns to the tomb, possibly at night. This concept of the soul differs widely from the Judeo-Christian concepts, except for this ability of the ba to fly out into daylight and return to the dark tomb at night. This stark contrast may have given rise to the Christian concept of the soul going either to heaven or hell with the added monocultural or one-sided perception that it is one or the other.

CHAPTER 57

My Story

Part 1: Am I Alone? The Facts

I mentioned Bruce Lipton's book, *The Biology of Belief.* After I had read as much as I dared about Quantum Physics, I read Lipton's book. At that time, I was already convinced that I was not alone, and that somehow, somewhere, I am connected with everyone and everything. Lipton provided the scientific basis for that theory (or belief).

In *The Biology of Belief,* Lipton illustrates a human cell enlarged to the point where I could see all the sensory bumps and follicles on it. Lipton says that a single cell is the microcosm, while the human body is the macrocosm.

'That's it!' I thought to myself. Weighing in at approximately 200 lbs, I might carry as many as three hundred trillion cells. (Some authorities claim we only have 100 trillion.) What I am interested in is this: if every cell has up to two-dozen sensors, my body has the use of 2.4 quadrillion sensors to suss out the world—even the universe—while I am alive and conscious.

Another way of looking at these vast numbers is that among my 100 trillion cells, I have 14,285 cells for each human being on the surface of this planet. No matter how I look at it, I have the sensory capacity to be in 'contact' with every human being who is alive at any given time in my life. I cannot possibly be alone.

Judgment

The well-known Biblical adage, "Judge not, lest you be judged," seems to carry little or no weight. Judgments and prejudices rule.

I have placed 'prejudice' together with 'judgment' because of our daily use of both. There are times we expect a judgment to be a reasoned opinion. If it comes from a court of law, or from judges in a contest or at court, such consideration may be possible. But ordinary people make judgments hundreds of times daily and chances are that few of these receive any thought or consideration. My own judgments are most likely to be habitual likes or dislikes, or they may be based on my unconscious fears and prejudices.

So, what are prejudices? The Oxford dictionary defines 'prejudice' as "preconceived opinion that is not based on reason or actual experience."

There is no such thing as a well-reasoned prejudice! The question that comes to me is, "Is there a well-reasoned fear?" I don't think so. There are only unexplored fears. Personal judgments most likely fall into this same 'unexplored' category. Unexplored prejudices, unfortunately, are based on unexplored fears!

The dictionary definition offers us either reason or experience to apply to prejudices—or both. Reason resides in the head, experience in the body. I cannot expect a judge sitting on his bench to apply his experience to making a judgment. Someone who is xenophobic, however, would definitely benefit from the physical experience of living in a radically different culture in order to change that prejudice into a considered judgment. Such a person may still not like people from a foreign culture at the end of his or her stay, but at least the judgement would be 'considered'.

Am I responsible for my judgments and prejudices? If I keep on making judgments and applying my prejudices unconsciously, then no. Either I am not responsible for these sentiments, or I am not acting responsibly! It may not matter as long as I don't do anything about my judgments and prejudices. But when I participate in evicting a 'different looking' family from the neighborhood because I fear their presence will drive house values down, it definitely matters. It may look like I have a good reason for my prejudice, but it is unfounded and, in the end, such action based on an unexamined prejudice can be socially harmful

There is no proof behind any of my prejudices! There is only unconsciousness. I project my fears and insecurities onto the world around me, usually indiscriminately.

Emotional Reconnection

Part 1: The Story

In the Jungian mirror what I see in others is what I don't want to see in myself.

Several times in my life I have been approached by someone and asked to help a third party. For some reason, I said "Yes!" each time. And each time I got burned.

Both before and after my marriage, I found a home that was slightly larger than what I needed. Sometimes there was an extra room for a study. Other times I had set up a library with a comfortable leather chair and dreamed I was a rich man in a million-dollar mansion. Inevitably, there was also an extra room with a bed for visiting guests.

It was that extra bed that drew in the requests for a favor. Someone needed a temporary shelter, and each time I said, "OK, you can stay with me for a few days." The few days turned into a few weeks, and the few weeks into a few months. The temporary shelter became a permanent hideout. My goodwill was taken advantage of and I became offended and hurt. This is the story. But if I apply Dr. Gabor Maté's process of Compassionate Inquiry, the story has nothing to do with the problem. Telling the story is simply a step in the healing process. Telling the story is especially important when someone carries a belief that started in early childhood: not being heard, or not being loved.

Emotional Reconnection

Part 2: Applying the Compassionate Inquiry Process

I was so intent on telling my story to anyone who would listen, most likely because of my overwhelming need to be heard, that I completely missed the point that my story covered up MY problem: the childhood belief that I am not heard, therefore I am not loved. My listeners missed it too! The story worked for my listeners, but backfired on me. I missed my own role in it. I failed to see that I was the one who had exposed my insecurities by offering safe shelter to others. I wanted to be liked!

One interpretation of the story is that I attracted people who needed shelter. By giving people shelter, I may have unconsciously hoped to be liked, even loved. But once people had shelter, they would naturally want to keep it-stay in my extra room-in order to remain in their safe place. Insecurity does not allow people to see the larger picture. They never thought, "Do I inconvenience my host?"

Is there another interpretation? Yes, there is. It's that people sense I am a soft touch and can easily be persuaded to help others. Unfortunately, once I lose control of the situation, I blame others.

In the court of emotional wellness, I am on trial, because I am the one who hides my emotions when I blame others, when I make judgments, and when I complain that I am not heard, again and again! I created these belief systems unconsciously in my childhood precisely because no child can live with conflicting emotions.

But there is no court. Emotions are neither right nor wrong. They are what they are. What emotions did my guests' behavior trigger in me that I could neither see nor face when I was interacting with them?

At the time, I could not even go to my emotions! My first projection was to have empathy for anyone who had lost control over the course of their own life and ended up needing shelter at my home. It was a projection because of two things. First, because I had no compassion for myself. I could only feel sorry for the 'unfortunate'. Second, because I 'saw' the other person's insecurities, but not my own. My belief was that a person can lose interest in their own life and leave everything up to fate. My judgment was immediate! Although I felt sorry, I lost respect for such a person.

When I turn that criticism back onto myself, I have to ask myself this question: 'Was there a time in my life when I drifted at the mercy of fate, or even at the mercy of all three Fates? Was there a time in my life when I could not get up either the courage or the intent to steer my life in a certain direction? Do I remember a time when I could not take enough interest in my own life to form a goal, or to weave my own vision of what I wanted to be when I grew up?'

In other words, was there a time in my life when I did not respect myself for the very 'sins' that I now see in others?

There sure was!

My Story

Part 1: A Life of Emptiness: The Facts

I remember a day in Philadelphia in October of 1968. I was 24. I had just rented a stark corner of a rooming house near Independence Square. For the first time in my life I didn't have anything to do, I didn't have anyone to tell me or even advise me what the next step was.

OK, that is not technically true. The last person I saw before being discharged from the US Army told me about my temporary unemployment benefits and that I should get a job.

I sat on the single bed, provided by the landlord, because the chair was too uncomfortable. I stared at the wall and asked myself, "How did I get here?"

I felt nothing.

My 'analysis' was a simple set of horizontal, sequential events.

I had six years of 'childhood' to begin with, during which time I absorbed everything I saw, heard and experienced. It was a time that Carolyn Myss calls the 'tribal instruction'. It was followed by sixteen years of schooling and two years of military service. The first seven years of schooling took place in Budapest, Hungary, and the next nine in Pennsylvania. My military service was in the US Army, and all Stateside.

What is wrong with this picture? Nothing. If I was 'fated' to be well educated and to serve my country, I had the best education money could buy, and the best military postings anyone could want.

It wasn't even 'my' money that paid for my education. I was on a four-year full scholarship with a stipend at the University of Pennsylvania. My role was to keep up a standard so that I don't lose that scholarship. And I did just that.

I had no role in where I was assigned during my military service. Yet, I had a rich experience serving at Fort Myer, Virginia, with the Third Battalion, Third Brigade—The Old Guard, providing honor guard services to those Viet Nam casualties who were buried at Arlington National Cemetery. In sum, there is no higher honor and respect one can pay to fellow Americans.

The only thing wrong with this picture, perhaps, was that I did not "choose" to do any of these. It all "happened" to me. While I was going through these experiences, I was emotionally vacant. Yes, I was happy and sad, joyful and depressed, scared and enthusiastic in any given situation. But in some sense, "I" wasn't there. All my emotions were reactions to outside events and activities.

My Story

Part 2: Emotional Absence: Dumb Luck or Fate or Divine Guidance?

Here is one simple example. During my freshman year at Penn, I received a letter asking me to choose my major. I had to ask my room-mate what a 'major' was. He told me, "It was the subject you like best, or the subject that brings you the best grade." I was satisfied with that response because Political Science fit both of these descriptions.

All I 'knew' in the larger scheme of things was that I had to maintain a 2.0 average in order to keep my scholarship. That is what I concentrated on for four years, and received my A.B. with something like a 2.0009 average. I kept busy, and had my share of romances, angst, fraternity life, music and art. I don't remember feeling anything else but pain or pleasure.

I did not tell my mother my grade average, only the victory of graduation. She had invited me to the Mediterranean island of Malta where she had met an Englishman and they planned to marry. I attended the wedding. After that, my family sent me to Paris, France for the summer of 1966 to live on $5.00 per day. It was an adventure. In September, the

Selective Service Board required me to come home and get on a troop-carrier train to Fort Jackson.

It was an active two years in the US Army. I showed leadership qualities, which I quickly squashed because it brought too much work. I learned to manipulate the system to my advantage and carve out a sense of freedom within a closed, authoritarian system. There was one underlying emotion: fear. It was the fear of getting caught, the fear of being sent to Viet Nam, and the fear of being robbed by fellow soldiers. The entire system was running on fear. Yes, I must have experienced all the other emotions as well, but they remained unconscious. Even my fledgling poetry career at the time focused on fear.

Eventually I received orders to go to Viet Nam. I took the 30-day leave the US Army offered, and flew to Europe to say good-bye to my mother and stepfather and my father.

I returned to Fort Jackson and reported to the assigned barracks on a Friday night. I registered with the duty sergeant and settled on a bunk for five minutes. Figuring the army did not work on weekends, I took a bus into Philadelphia where I had friends. I returned to the barracks Sunday night. The barracks were still empty.

Fear and adrenalin filled my body. My perception, which was influenced by a large dose of naiveté that accompanied me throughout my life, was that something was wrong. The empty barracks raised a flag in my mind.

I went to the duty sergeant, the same person I saw on Friday night, and asked, "Where is everybody?"

He looked at me smugly and said, "In Viet Nam! Where were you?"

I said, "In Philadelphia."

"You were AWOL," he said, leaning back on his chair.

"Yes," I admitted and squeaked in a lame explanation. "In a year of service nobody did anything on weekends. So I went to Philadelphia."

"I could send you to Leavenworth for that," the staff sergeant mused. I offered no resistance. I just stood there frozen with fear. "But you are here," he continued. "I'll just put you in with the next batch."

The next morning, with the barracks full of men, we were marched around to pick up our 'Viet Nam gear.' On one of the marches I asked if there was a 'complaints desk'. Without any ado, a corporal led me to a large tent with at least 12 temporary desks staffed with clerks, Army Regulations books and telephones. They were all doing a brisk business.

When my turn came, I complained that with only eight months left of my tour of duty, I did not qualify for the regulation nine months of service required to go and fight in Viet Nam. With great apologies, the clerk informed me that the Army Regulations had changed that service time to six months, and therefore, I was totally eligible.

"Anything else?"

It occurred to me that my father was alive and well, living in Budapest, Hungary.

"Can you prove it?" the clerk asked.

"It's on my personal data sheet you're holding."

In its wisdom, the US Army had devised a single page form, an MOS, that held one's vital information. The clerk read the form and said, "I have to call a Major in the Pentagon." He picked up the telephone, repeated the information, listened and said, "Yes, Sir!" He hung up the telephone, looked up at me and asked, "Where would you like to go? Any US Army base anywhere in the world is open to you. You are not eligible to go to Viet Nam!"

CHAPTER

63

My Story

Part 3: The Interpretation

Sitting on my bed, staring at a stark, undecorated wall near the birthplace
of the United States (Independence Hall in Philadelphia, Pennsylvania)
I had a chance to contrast the decision I made as a freshman student at
Penn about what my major would be with the decision I would soon be
making as to what work I would take. Choosing a major had happened in
an academic context, almost like choosing an item on a restaurant menu.
As far as I could see, it was part of the minutia of my education, not a career
choice as it would be for some students. I was either not mature enough to
see the larger picture, or I was not raised to be aware of the larger picture.
My parents lived under Communism in survival mode. Chances are that
I was mostly living in survival mode also. My choice of Political Science
as a major meant that I became an 'expert' on Sino-Soviet relationships in
the 1950s. What now? With a 2.0 average, I could enter neither graduate
school nor any of the "think tanks" I had dreamed about.

There are many ways of looking at myself. I present myself in these stories as having been emotionless and clueless. And I was. At the same time, 'emotionless' and 'clueless' are interpretations, or perspectives. I was simply not connected to my core feelings. I did not know I was emotionless and clueless. I thought I was perfectly normal. In some sense, I was just that!

After being discharged from the US Army I hung around downtown Philadelphia for a few weeks. I wanted to 'feel' what it meant to be unemployed. Of course, I now know that the meaning of being unemployed is not a feeling. More likely, I wanted to experience the state of being unemployed.

What does an unemployed person do with his time? I walked Market Street, drank one cup of coffee after another, ate cheap Chinese food and waited.

Then I went to a head-hunting firm and took the first job they offered me. It was another unconscious "menu" choice.

"This sounds like an interesting job. Let's take it!"

Spiritual teachers talk about a part of every person that is untouched by the pain and suffering of life. This part, whether I call it my Soul, a unique, personalized energy field, an inner knowing core, or by any other name, is connected either to God, if I am religious, or to the Universe, if I follow Quantum Physics and Entanglement. Among meditators and spiritual students, this part of human beings is either divine, or is connected to divinity. "Divine" and "divinity", of course, correspond to that aspect of Quantum Fields where the sole purpose of their existence is to return to balance. I cannot prove that a Quantum Field's automatic return to balance is the same as the Christian ideal of living a life of love, but both love and balance are unconditional.

Emotional Reconnection

Part 4: Connecting with My Pain

This recollection of my youth has been a current part of an ongoing attempt to face my own pain. I had motivation. I had attended four Compassionate Inquiry workshops with Dr. Gabor Maté, two in person in Toronto, Ontario, and two on-line during 2017-18. I saw the 'value' in going where most people don't dare to go: to face my pain.

The last thing people want to do is to face their pain. The standard response to pain is to blame it on someone else or soothe it with addictive behavior or substances.

In April, 2018, I started studying and practicing for a certification in the Compassionate Inquiry process. Session after Compassionate Inquiry practice session I refused to connect with my pain, my fears, or my anger. I simply could not see or feel any. It took me nearly eight months of encouragement from other Compassionate Inquiry practitioners to lower my guard, allow myself to become vulnerable, and begin to sense that there were deeply repressed, painful feelings bottled up in me.

I had tears in my eyes when I first realized that these fears had played me all my life. I clearly saw their 'work' in my relationships with people. The closer I came to someone, and the more intimate the relationship became, the more defenses I built around myself.

I know. I am not the only one to have responded to life by building defensive walls. But here was a valuable lesson. I had to reinvent the wheel. I could not benefit from, or take over someone else's wheel. There is so much conventional wisdom "out there", why not just learn from it?

I did learn as much as I could from as many people as I could. I amassed a great knowledge base and used it with a good dose of native intelligence. But I was still as dumb as a doornail: emotionally. Recognizing my emotional disconnection from my authenticity is not an intellectual exercise. Emotional reconnection was and is not a matter of book learning and reasoning things out. It is a life experience.

Everyone should know about separation (not just church from state) but reason from emotion. Whenever someone becomes emotionally overexcited, the hippocampus shuts down, and reason stops. Perhaps in my own unconsciousness I never noticed that. Yet, this separation between emotions and reason is often evident. When a police officer stops a vehicle and the person behind the wheel is very scared, that person will not find the right words to say, will often be unable to find the right documents, or will say the most ridiculous things. Some people who find themselves unexpectedly in front of an audience, freeze. They are so afraid that no words will come out of their mouth!

Tracking my emotions may register in my intellect, but when I feel the pain of my two-year-old childhood self manifest in me now, there is no rational response. There is only amazement and self-compassion. How did my two-year-old self hold on to that pain for so many years? What can I do for such a child as I used to be? There is only one way to deal with such a discovery within me, and that is to give that child what it needed, what it still needs, what it did not get from my care-givers: love and compassion. That is the connection.

For me, making connection with my inner pain brought a unique set of rewards: a growing self-confidence, the ability to relate to others more clearly and even authentically, and a sense of inner happiness, perhaps the result of having more oxytocin released into my bloodstream.

CHAPTER

65

Emotional Reconnection

Part 5: Where Does my Pain Take Me?

Practicing Compassionate Inquiry upon myself pointed me to my own unconsciousness. I acknowledged a deep sense of emptiness within me from having had no say over my own existence during the first twenty-five years of my life. The fear itself was primal. It came from my childhood when even the disappearance of my mother, however temporary, sent me into survival mode and the fear that I would die. It is little wonder, then, that later on in life I was afraid I would lose interest in living and therefore die.

Dr. Gabor Maté, however, repeats in his talks and teachings that it was the child I remember being, who was powerless and helpless. In adulthood I replay those childhood belief systems over and over again. Each replay intensifies the pain. I blame each new circumstance, and each person who happens to be near me, as being responsible for my fears and pain. Unconsciousness inhibits responsibility.

I had no idea that it was as a child that I first experienced the feeling of being scared to death. Oddly enough it was not just me as a child who was really scared to death! It was everyone around me, huddled in a dark bomb shelter! As an infant, I picked up these feelings from my mother and my environment. However, in order to stay alive, I suppressed that fear.

Once I was old enough to speak, other fears arose that caused me deep pain. One fear came from a belief that, since my parents did not hold me when I needed to be held, did not meet my needs, they did not love me. In response, I created the belief that I was not lovable! Yet, they thought (and my mother once told me so when, as an adult, I berated her for her lack of parenting skills) that they had done their best!

My parents assured me that I was a quiet infant and toddler, however I was constantly sick and feverish. I caught every childhood disease that went around the neighborhood plus the whooping cough. Perhaps I had wanted to get rid of this body that was emotionally betraying me.

As a child, I had no idea that I had lost connection with my authentic self, and given up my authenticity for the sake of keeping the attachment to my parents. But that is what happened. My life as a child was a simple survival response of a dependent to everything that went wrong; to all my needs that could not be met And my survival response was to freeze and to repress my fears and anger!

Emotional Reconnection

Part 6: What Happens to the Pain?

By 1968, when I sat in that stark room in Philadelphia, the realization that I lacked self-respect was no longer a life-and-death matter. But I didn't know that then. I suppressed my feelings. I suppressed my feelings, because that is what I was used to doing ever since my childhood.

I worked for five years, during which my company took me to cities of the eastern US, Canada, England and France as a consultant. My specialty was helping corporate data entry operations change from manual entry to computer entry. I loved the travel, but found the work utterly boring.

That boredom led me to my first life-changing decision: to study Ancient Egyptian Language and Literature. The decision evolved slowly. Ever since my university days I saw a linear connection between my "Western" Judeo-Christian religious culture and ancient Egypt. Moses came from Egypt, David escaped to Egypt, Jesus was taken to Egypt to save his life when King Herod ordered the murder of all children one year old or younger.

I also saw a linear connection between my "Western" philosophical tradition and ancient Egypt. I noticed that Solon spoke highly of the Egyptians. He said the Greeks were like children in comparison! Thales learned mathematics from the Egyptians, and Pythagoras spent over twenty years living and studying in Egypt. It was as if these Greek Philosophers all bragged about how many years they had spent in Egypt studying ancient wisdom. I asked myself the question, "What did the ancient Egyptians know that was so valuable to both Moses (and his people) and Pythagoras (and his fellow philosophers)?

This question also took my mind off my pain.

Fast forwarding to the here-and-now, I know that I am not in a life-and-death survival situation when I face emotional pain. I also have the additional knowledge of the tools of the Compassionate Inquiry process to help me face that pain. By facing it, like looking a demon in the eyes, the pain loses its 'eternal' appearance and disappears. I have found a way to cope with my pain.

Emotional pain, however, does not just stop. My life is filled with stressful moments, and each stress is able to re-trigger the pain. I have not 'healed' the pain, but I have learned to cope with it. Each time stress brings emotional upset and pain, I know I can 'handle' it. Sometimes it is as simple as going within myself and breathing deeply, and reminding myself that there is no pain in the present moment. This reality has become the foundation of the process of mindfulness.

Other times, I bring to mind the hurt child I used to be and reassure him that he is in a safe place at the moment, held in love and compassion by our shared emotional core!

Emotional Reconnection

Part 7: I Choose a Meaningful Discipline

I breathe, therefore, I am!

Most of my life I have taken my breathing for granted. It is true that my gym teachers preached the benefits of deep breathing, and that my father took the family on long walks every Sunday and repeatedly told me to breathe in for four steps, and breathe out for four steps. It is true that my meditation in a Rosicrucian Lodge involved the practice of taking long, slow, deep breaths, and that one alternative health practitioner said that the lungs needed to be refreshed every seven hours by exhaling every last bit of stale air and replenishing it with fresh air, but still, I have largely taken my breathing for granted.

In 2015 I had embarked on the Beyond Addiction Program: the Yogic Way of Recovery.

I was not an alcoholic, nor even a drug user. Before the course, I attended a workshop and was surprised when Dr. Maté talked about his addictions as a workaholic and a classical record or CD collector. As he worked with Vancouver east side addicts, and told them of his inability to pass a music store without spending hundreds of dollars on CDs, his patients nodded their heads and said, "Yeah, Doc, you are just like us." Those heroin addicts recognized the addictions and did not make any class distinctions. Emotions, like addictions, make no class-distinctions.

If I am not conscious of a recurring, habitual action that slowly but surely destroys or negatively influences my life, I am being guided—nay, driven—by that addiction. Unfortunately for me, even my habituated responses to my children, my loved ones, my coworkers or those who work for me (any response that is not mindful, but, rather, brings conflict or self-sabotage into my life) can be an addiction!

However, Dr. Maté says that, "not all compulsive, repetitive behaviors are addictions. Addictions involve temporary craving, relief, and pleasure. Many compulsive negative behaviors are not addictions, but, rather, forms of coping."

Who knew there is so much to learn?

The Beyond Addiction Program uses Kundalini Yoga as the discipline that can connect me with my repressed emotions. As with any form of yoga, it teaches breathing techniques, called 'pranayama'.

Since most of my life I was "down-and-out" in the emotional sense, breathing was not a concern for me. It was autonomic; I didn't have to worry about it. I didn't have to be conscious of it. Kundalini Yoga, however, demanded that I pay attention to my breath. So I took a deep breath. And then I took another. I chose to breathe deeply, slowly, for five or six minutes during the pranayama, then remained aware of my breathing throughout the Kundalini Yoga practice.

Yes, there was resistance! For the first year I only practiced once a week, and only when I met with another practitioner who was willing to guide me. Then yoga and the breathing became a daily practice for me for the next two years. It brought me a sense of accomplishment, physical health, and inner satisfaction.

With those deep breaths I started to take interest in my own life.

One of the basic practices of Kundalini Yoga is to stop after each three, or five, or ten minute practice and feel what is going on in the body. By the end of those three years of practice, I was reconnecting with my authentic feelings.

CHAPTER

68

Emotional Reconnection

Part 8: Recap and Reconnection

I was born in 1944. I was "born again," following other boys and girls down a church aisle to 'accept Jesus into my heart,' in 1960. I was born into my career as an "Egyptologist" in 1973. For the first time in my life I was emotionally connected with what I was doing and I was studying for myself. I began to have respect for myself. But I wasn't conscious of being emotionally connected to my authentic self. I figured I had a Soul, but I did not have to deal with it. It looked after itself. I did not yet know that the Soul actually guided my life, whether I was conscious of it or not.

I had help, though. When I was 32, and still unmarried, an Anthroposophical mentor told me that it's OK to exercise my feelings on a daily basis, but not notice their cumulative effect! He also warned me that, at some point, I would begin to feel a yearning for the constant company of a woman, and not just for sexual satisfaction.

He gave me this advice; I would have to make myself available to women I was attracted to. I would have to let them know I was interested.

However, I would have to let them make the decision as to whether or not they would date me, get to know me, or marry me.

I did not know it at the time, but I had begun the process of calling on my 'inner guide'—my slowly building connection to my authentic emotional self—to run my life on the basis of that inner guidance instead of leaving it up to fate!

Spiritual teachers say that our inner guide has never left us. Dr. Maté makes a perfect case for the fact that our naturally occurring fetal and childhood traumas forced us to disconnect from that authentic 'self'. (See his reference to A.H. Almaas on p. 48)

My parents and environment looked after my physical needs, but did not nurture or meet the needs of my authenticity and its guidance. As a result, I developed a series of coping mechanisms to bring back whatever it is that I had lost. An infant cannot know nor communicate what it truly needs. Parents and caregivers who had never had their needs met, cannot possibly meet my needs at this time either! Not having my needs met threatened my survival. That threat sent me into survival response. I froze and suppressed my need to be loved. I developed coping strategies to renew connection, or attachment at the loss of my authenticity. Those coping mechanisms developed my 'personality'. And it is my personality that now gets in the way of my emotional reconnection. I am so attached to my personality, that I will not give up the adaptations I developed as a child in order to begin an emotional development that was not completed in childhood.

I reviewed these stages of my life inadvertently when I told stories (and continue to do so with the stories included in this book) to whoever would listen.

As an aside, there is a notion in Freemasonry that we are each searching for something that way lost. The usual consensus is that it is knowledge. I propose, though, that is it is our authenticity. What we lost is our connection to our soul.

From the moment I entered the certification course for Compassionate Inquiry, I began to apply the Compassionate Inquiry practice to myself.

What was my motivation to tell this story or that? I began to see and feel my fear, my anger and my pain. I was able to accept that all these emotions have been carefully stored out of my sight, repressed, and unconscious, since my childhood. These are also my current fears, angers and pain, which I had unconsciously carried all my life, including the pain of my fetus cringing from my mother's stresses. I carry the fear of people who were around me when I was six months old, people who feared for their own lives. I carry the anger of my father who beat me for non-compliance because his father had beaten him for the same thing.

Each stress in my life re-kindled and re-animated this fear, anger and pain until recently, when I began to see these repressed feelings for what they are. I was able to face them, and accept them. In the process I was able to accept myself and examine the beliefs that I had made up about myself as a child. If in my childhood I had decided that I was not lovable, I can now reverse that decision. I can authentically tell that childhood 'self' within me that I am lovable. Although my parents were not able to extend the kind of love I had needed as a child, I can now take the role of my parents and provide the child I was with what he needed but did not receive.

If I believe I am not good enough, all I have to do is look at my accomplishments. It might take the rest of my life to ferret out other repressed emotions, but I am reconnecting with my authentic self. I am not afraid of showing my vulnerabilities. I have learned new and useful coping skills.

Emotional Reconnection

Part 9: Lesson and Takeaway

What was my motivation for telling my stories in the first place? I needed attention,

I likely learned to tell my stories quite young. I was raised in a story-telling environment. In spite of all the needs my parents could not fulfill, they told me stories, read me stories and encouraged me to begin to make up my own stories. As I grew up, I simply turned to other people either to hear their stories, or to tell mine. I was not yet aware that I had been living at the mercy of fate. Because of my ignorance, I projected myself into my stories without having any respect for my own character.

I developed my character as someone who was operating unconsciously. I painted him as a person who was emotionally disconnected from his own life. As I was describing myself, I believed I had painted a quaint picture of an innocent boy holding his head high even while being buffeted by every wind and nearly overwhelmed by every wave!

A few years ago, when I discovered that all these stories were covering up a deeper, emotional pain, it was a 'revelation'. I was filled with gratitude that the emotional reconnection was possible, and that it had begun within me. I learned or applied (or both) a measure of compassion for myself when I noticed that I had none for my fictional character!

Of course, I have even more to learn. When I do, I'll write another book.

Do I Have to Be Responsible for Myself?

Part 1: What About My 'Comfort Zone'?

Life Coaches and yoga teachers tend to say what athletic and gym coaches hold dear: "Push past your comfort level."

As people age, they tend to say, "Oh, I am slowing down. I can no longer do this. I can no longer do that ..."

Of course, I don't need to age to get to that point. I can become aware of slowing down at any stage in life, especially if I have been carrying long-term inflammatory conditions inside my body, or other chronic 'dis-eases'. But I also slow down when I stop exercising—when I stop pushing myself past my comfort zone.

And that's the key: to be able to accept a few moments of discomfort. I didn't say pain! It's just the feeling of slight discomfort. I can climb a few more steps today than I did yesterday. I can walk a few more blocks than I think I can do. I can eat one hamburger instead of two and downsize the French Fries. Or replace the beef burger with a Portobello Mushroom burger.

Where do I get the motivation to break out of my comfort zone? As a child, a toddler, neurobiological researchers tell me, there was an internal urge to explore and overcome obstacles. OK, I might not remember that urge, because very few of us remember our childhood prior to reaching our fourth year. It is a matter of the hippocampus developing our memory. Prior to age four when explicit memory develops, most children cannot remember what happened to them. The memory is there, but it is implicit memory.

Psychotherapists are fond of reminding us that for most of us, our personality had fully formed by age two. We might not remember anything about how that personality was forged, which was most likely through an endless series of painful adaptations and inadvertent search for coping skills, but our personality comes through at any given moment in our adult life. And that personality we display is the embodiment of our pre-verbal memory.

I have read enough childhood brain development books to know (and remember) that after his or her survival needs are met (food, clothing and shelter), the next phase of the toddler stage takes the child past the comfort zone. Big time!

Joseph Chilton Pearce, in his book, *The Magical Child*, tells us the neuroscience research that the purpose of life for the toddler is to explore and overcome obstacles. It is not a choice or a decision. It is an inner drive. People call it the 'terrible twos', thus completely mistaking the child's needs. Pearce gives the example of a toddler reaching for a precious object that the parents have left within reach. The mother keeps saying, "Don't touch that! Don't touch that!" But the toddler's drive to explore is strong. The child has no concept of why the mother would be saying "no". He or she reaches for that object.

What's going on? Here is this person who is supposed to be my ally, who usually feeds and comforts me, but now turns on me and betrays me! Instead of putting that precious object out of the child's reach, parents become fixated on teaching their child to obey. At the toddler stage, children need to learn about their surroundings. That is their natural drive.

When did we lose that internal drive? It doesn't matter. This loss may be partially due to the parents' ignorance of childhood development. It may be due to the pedagogic implementation of "breaking the child's will." It is part of our socialization.

Very few of us are curious enough to get past our comfort zone. (See Chapter 83 for another take on 'comfort zone')

Do I Have to Be Responsible for Myself?

Part 2: What About my Food?

For whatever reason, I used to believe that the various levels of our government looked after my best interests. I mean, I was sure that all the certifications, inspections, supervision and licensing ensured that all my food was safe to eat. Health professionals like medical doctors, Public Health Units, Nutritionists and others would notify me, and the rest of the public when something needs to be changed or avoided. And, to a certain extent, they do. Unfortunately I mostly hear about health concerns involving my food after a few thousand people have been poisoned and there is a public recall.

What governments, public agencies and professionals do is not enough. Corporate lobbying has changed the game and now government agencies tend to follow corporate guidance as to what is edible. Finding healthy food has become 'my' responsibility—if I care to take it.

A century or two ago, 95% of all the population lived on the land and farmed it. What they ate was not a problem. Today, 97% of us live in urban or suburban settings in North America and Europe. Food would still not be a problem, except that the 3% who are doing the food growing are largely doing it chemically, toxically, and often inhumanely. Industrial farming is based on monocrop management with glyphosate-infused herbicide sprays and chemical fertilizers. It brings us food, but that food is often toxic and lacks nutrition.

As a result, I have to become a researcher. My kitchen has to transform into a laboratory. My head has to turn into an encyclopedia in order for me to know what is good for me and what is not. I have to learn to discern what will lead to better health rather than slow me down and inevitably cause me to develop disease. Death may be inevitable (though lots of people challenge it) but wellness is an art I can practice until I am too tired to keep it up.

If the government and its agencies are no longer responsible for the purity of my food, what else can I do? If I don't take on that responsibility, I will expose myself to long-term harm. The body, mind and emotions are totally interactive. I harm one, the other two will manifest the change as well. As more and more evidence comes in showing that repressed, unresolved emotional trauma has 'side effects', such as chronic body responses and inflammation, higher body-toxicity likely has a dampening effect on my emotions. We'll let the researchers have the last say on that topic.

Vulnerability

Part 1: What Do I do When I Feel Vulnerable?

Vulnerability is part of my healing.

In spite of that possibility, it is one of those counter-intuitive perspectives I fail to examine. It is easier to avoid thinking about it altogether.

I say 'perspective' or a state of being, because vulnerability is not a feeling. If I have to be honest with myself (and really, that is the only useful choice) I have to accept and acknowledge that behind the concept of 'vulnerability' is a feeling of fear. Vulnerability and insecurity could be interchangeable, except that insecurity encompasses so much more than just vulnerability.

What is going on?

On the one hand, I am taught to hide my vulnerabilities because people will shame me for them; bullies will take advantage of me because of them. On the other hand, Life and Business Coaches tell me to hang them out to dry, and in public. Once everyone knows I am being neurotic, or having episodes of paranoia, and that I am OK with that, then no one can do anything about it because:

1. I am no longer bothered.

2. Now they are the ones who are hiding or repressing the same vulnerability and fear that I will see right through them.

3. Somehow, my public vulnerability has transmogrified into a strength that bullies and gossips fear.

This change from a repressed, guarded and seemingly shameful sense of being vulnerable to an open, unguarded, acknowledged and accepted one also offers a role model to those bullies and gossips. Role modeling, for some reason, teaches people far better than talking, counseling or reading. It is a matter of efficiency. In fact, role modeling seems to be the most efficient teaching tool not only in dealing with my fear of vulnerability, but also in dealing with most other uncomfortable feelings.

Vulnerability

Part 2: Can I Be Assertive and Resentful at the Same Time?

Of course I can. It is not a useful state of being, if only because resentment is still, and always will be self-harming.

So here is the story of Joe and Jill (not their real names).

I met Joe at the age of seventy, during the time he had decided to leave his wife and family in order to find himself. Joe was not a novice. He was a serious meditator, a long-distance runner, and had followed pop-psychology most of his life.

We met to discuss our personal spiritual-emotional progress. What I did not realize, at first, was that he presented only his best side to me. At the time, I was already aware that authenticity was a combination of self-acceptance and vulnerability. It became evident to me that he was hiding his vulnerabilities even as I was practicing to open myself to mine.

His wife and son arrived, and we decided to go out for dinner to a quiet restaurant. During dinner conversation I casually mentioned to Jill, Joe's wife, that Joe and I had been talking about their impending separation.

There was deadly silence at first. But Jill found her strength and began to speak, saying that Joe had "no balls" when it came to making household decisions. That remark caught Joe off guard. He had told me that he didn't make such decisions because he had handed the financial and household matters over to Jill. He figured that since she was financing most of it, she could also make most of the decisions.

In one sense, he trusted Jill's decisions. He had told me that her decisions were always for the benefit of the whole family. Joe did not see it coming that his stepping back from household decisions would be interpreted by his wife as "having no balls!"

While we were talking just between the two of us, I had completely accepted Joe's explanation at face value. I had done the very same thing with my ex-wife! I let her make most household decisions precisely because she financed them. But when Jill shared her perspective, I realized that the last seven to ten years of my marriage, I had also showed "no balls". I was even scared of leaving the marriage because I did not know how I would survive. I had assets, but my wife earned cash.

In one sense, Jill was assertive and spoke her truth. If she had stopped there, I would have learned nothing. But Jill did not stop. She continued to say that she had supported Joe for 45 years, and had no objection to his leaving to find himself ("whatever that means," she added), but that she refused to support him any further.

A highly placed official in public service, Jill had become resentful. As far as she could see, Joe had decided to "abandon" her and their grown-up children.

I could see at once that the interpretation of being abandoned brought out deep seated fears, which Jill had never faced. But, Jill continued. She held Joe responsible for how she felt and she resented it.

I was not yet trained to ask her if she was willing to go into her state of abandonment and search what childhood survival fears it had activated in her. I was, however, able to tell Jill that "abandonment" was her perspective.

"I resent him leaving us!" she shot back!

Vulnerability

Part 3: Finding Anger and Fear

Jill found herself exposed and vulnerable by my dinner-table remarks. First, by the fact that Joe had told me about their impending separation, and second, by being surprised that I downgraded her 'feeling' of abandonment to a mere mental perspective.

But Jill was on a roll. She found her strength and lashed out against Joe. Then she turned to me and asked, "Is everything I said an 'interpretation' or am I expressing my true feelings?"

"In one word," I asked, "what is your true feeling?"

"I'm angry!" Jill said.

"That's a true feeling," I said. "And you have every right to feel angry."

It was Joe's turn to absorb the shock. He also felt vulnerable and exposed because his personal conversations with me now looked to be so one-sided. His wife had just attacked him and exposed him as indecisive. Joe had thought that he had rationalized his indecisiveness satisfactorily So her started again by explaining to Jill what he had explained to me earlier.

He fully trusted her decisions about the household. He was also honest and has been telling her all along that he felt this need to leave her and find himself. (Whatever that means).

Jill pounced on him at once. "And how are you going to finance a second household while you 'find yourself?'" she asked.

Joe hung his head. Jill had exposed his real fear. Now he had to admit it. "I was going to ask you to pay my rent for the first year."

Our table fell silent. Their son, in his early thirties, weighed in. "You are going to leave us, and you want Mom to pay for it? Isn't that like adding insult to injury?"

At this point the genuine love that Joe and Jill still shared came into play. Whatever vulnerability Jill may have felt, transformed into self-confidence and power. "I'll tell you what, Hon! I will do that. I will finance you fully for one year. But I will not have you crawling back after that. You want to be on your own, you be on your own."

Jill had balls. She found her strength. Rather than plead that her heart was broken, she made an offer from her adult, loving heart. She would deal with her issue of abandonment later.

What about Joe? Joe got exactly what he wanted. He told me afterwards that even though my dinner-table remark caught him off guard, his wife made a decision that was still the best for the entire family. He did not examine his dependence. He did not feel he had to deal with his vulnerability because he was not afraid of severing his connection with Jill. He was already connected to his meditation community, and so was not worried about being alone. "If connection in adulthood is the same need as being held is a need for an infant," Joe said, "then I feel connected and somehow believe that that connectedness trumps vulnerability."

CHAPTER

75

Who Will Hold Me?

Part 1: What Happens When I am Not Held as a Child?

I might benefit from gently asking myself, "What keeps me from being 'held' by my own inner resources?" Joe had felt connected, or 'held' by his support group, which was his meditation community.

Now I felt vulnerable. Coming out of that dinner with Joe and his family, I had to ask myself, "Who am I connected to? Who is 'holding' me?"

This question may involve several streams of knowledge. I am familiar with each of them.

One knowledge stream is that the most important need a newborn and pre-verbal child has is to be held. Attachment, or connection, for an infant, is a matter of survival. Mother puts her baby down to go to the bathroom, and the moment she disappears from sight, the baby goes into stress. This repeated separation ends up in the child internalizing the trauma of separation. But the separation trauma is not that the mother had disappeared. The separation trauma came when the child's stress (at its mother's disappearance) separated the child from his or her own authentic emotions!

It is a matter of physiology. When the mother goes out of sight, the infant does not see her. The infant does not have the ability to project the mother's presence elsewhere, nor to project her return. As far as the infant is concerned, the mother has disappeared. Mother is the source of food. The only need the infant can sense is being fed and being held.

Being fed and being held, when seemingly denied, become survival issues for an infant! When the infant is not held; when the infant loses contact with his or her mother or caregiver; when the infant 'loses sight' of the only source of food, the infant goes into stress and into survival mode.

Another knowledge stream is that the "personality" develops as the child has to separate from his or her own internal support resource: the infant's own emotional center, perhaps what Joseph Chilton Pearce had called "a heart-connection." What we call it doesn't matter, but each of us is born with this internal emotional resource and "it" never leaves us.

Even as my care-giver separates herself from me—puts me down into my crib and sweetly says goodnight—I go into stress. I don't have the means to say, "I need to be held!" But I need to be held! So I react not only outward, but also within me. I separate myself from my own inner emotional resource center. I begin to function in survival mode. I am left with a problem I cannot solve, "How do I bring back my source of food?"

As an infant, 'flight' is not available to me. As for 'fight', I might cry or scream for a while, flail my arms and legs, and breathe in panic mode. Chances are my parents were told to let me cry, and will not pick me up.

I have one more survival option, which is to freeze. I quiet down, and go into a trance. If I could think, I would most likely believe that I am going to die. These are the only coping mechanisms available to me for the survival issues that have just been sprung on me by my environment. I am not responsible for what my parents do with me. My parents are not responsible for what they do either, because they don't know any better. Our entire culture has accepted the brutalization of its children as a necessity.

Who Will Hold Me?

Part 2: When I Am an Adult?

It's not that my mother didn't love me. She probably did, and very deeply. But she needed to go to the bathroom. Or she needed some rest. She was certainly stressed. Her stress, for which she was not responsible, became my stress.

A third knowledge stream that is available to me comes from my current state of being, or state of mind. I am here as an adult, separated from my own inner emotional resources, but still carrying the pain of my pre-verbal childhood traumas. I have no explicit memory as to where my traumas originated. Left to my own devices as an adult, I tend to attribute my pain to external sources. Mostly, I blame others for my pain. Or, I feel shame for living with pain while everyone else seems to be living pain-free. That perception, of course, is totally mistaken!!! But that is where I am coming from.

The fact is, though, that my internal emotional core, my resource, although left 'undeveloped' since childhood, has not abandoned me. The innate goal of this emotional core is my ongoing well-being. While this core remained undeveloped because my emotional development was arrested by unresolved trauma, the potential connection, that is, the reconnection, remained open.

A fourth knowledge stream reminds me that, as a child, I was "attached" to my caregivers, so no matter how much they hurt me, that is, left me, or otherwise sent me into survival mode, I still went back to them, because I still depended on my caregivers for my survival. It was not love that kept me by my mother's apron strings as an infant. She was the only one who gratified all my needs, most of the time.

A friend showed me a photograph of her three-year-old son climbing over his seated father's shoulder. They were both grinning with great glee, the kind of picture that shows a healthy interaction between father and son. My friend, though, confessed that both she and her husband were frustrated by their child, and often lost their temper with his many needs. They not only yelled and screamed in their anger, but would beat their child for not 'behaving' the way they would have liked, which is to behave like an obedient dog.

This kind of child-raising happens in the best of families. In fact, it is more likely to happen when we define the 'best' families in terms of "wealth". The more socially self-conscious the family is, the more psychological bonds and boundaries they demand of their small children. It is not a surprise. Most societies want to control and predict how their individuals behave. The more fear and pain a family can instill in their children, the better behaved they will be as they grow up: and the more psychologically disturbed. Studies done on the effects of brutalization of adults show that adults accept brutalization and tend to show more loyalty to those who have brutalized them.

It turns out, that the client who remembers having a good childhood and insists that s/he comes from a 'good' family during a Compassionate Inquiry process is often actually gilding over a terrible childhood with a dysfunctional family! This socially accepted 'brutalization' has an unconscious purpose. It is perpetrated to keep the child from running away. The child is too scared of the outside world to escape. Who is going to 'hold' them? Children tend to accept brutalization, or any abuse, as love.

Love is what they need, and infants and toddlers cannot contrast what is happening to them with what should be happening to them.

Who is going to hold me? No one. That is the point where I tend to develop either social coping skills or enter a 'normal' life of dysfunctional social interaction. This is the point where I begin to develop addictions.

My support groups might hold me. I will ultimately accept my family because I am dependent on my parents. I will pretend my school 'holds' me, or my sports team 'holds' me, or my gang 'holds' me.

I will find my tribe to hold me, or support me.

Who Will Hold Me?

Part 3: When the Tribe Doesn't?

Joseph Chilton Pearce quotes an anthropological study in his book, *A Crack in the Cosmic Egg.* He mentions a wonderfully idyllic childhood development model tribe. The women carry their children tied to their body for the better part of three years and breast-feed them during that time, even while their children also eat food. But at the age of four, this tribe sends their trauma-free children to a neighboring tribe!

These children know no one in that other tribe! They are practically brutalized by strangers, then, after several months, sent home. Why? So these children will learn never to leave home again! It doesn't matter when the brutalization happens.

What becomes clear is that the family and the tribe has a repressed, unspoken fear that its 'members' will leave. The family or tribe will develop customs or games, or tell scary children's stories in order to instill in the child a fear and distrust of the outside world. But they do it unconsciously.

A fifth knowledge stream that can help me concerns my own adult unawareness. As an adult, my tribe does not usually depend on me for its immediate survival. Everyone carries their unspoken, unknown (repressed) and therefore unacknowledged trauma. In fact, this well-hidden pain drives us both individually and collectively.

I habitually turn on my best friends, colleagues and partners and blame them for my pain. I use the joys and pleasures of the outside world to help soothe my pain—hence my addictions. I soothe my pain unconsciously, whether I take substances, work too hard, need sex all the time, run five miles every time I am stuck for a feeling (or am struggling with a feeling) and so on.

The Tibetan Book of the Dead (or by any other name) simply points out that if I don't face my pain, it will become worse. The question then becomes, "How do I face my pain? Do I go to a therapist? Do I go to Thailand? Do I go to my lover?" All of these can be a support group or an addiction. What internal resource do I have that has always been there, that I am now adult enough, and am hurting enough to find again?

That inner resource is authenticity. It will hold me and emotionally anchor or stabilize me. Once I am anchored, I can turn to my friends and family to support my emotional wellness. If they cannot, then I have to find such friends who will!

Do I Need Healing?

Part 1: Cultural Roots of My Trauma

When I was studying the teachings of Ptah-Hotep, written c. 4500 years ago, Prof. Ronald J. Williams at the University of Toronto's Near Eastern Studies department, who was also an Anglican Priest, noted that people would not have written instructions on how to live a good life, if their contemporaries would have already been living a good life. These "wisdom literature" authors, which include the author of the Book of Ecclesiastes in the Old Testament, perceived that people were 'bad'— whatever that means. Either as moralists or prophets, they saw that things could get better, if only....

That is where Moses and the Ten Commandments came in. If only you loved God; if only you didn't murder your fellow human being; if only you didn't have sex with your neighbor's wife without your neighbor's permission, or the consent of both, and so on, all would be well.

Moses distilled the hundreds of problems the ancient Egyptians had identified (one chapter in the Egyptian Book of the Dead lists 150 'do nots') into the Ten Commandments. He wanted to make it simple for his people.

The sheer strength of ten basic rules shows just how emotionally unstable, or mentally ill his people were. (Or, we all are!)

In European spirituality, women who were in touch with their own authentic emotional heart center and gut feelings, or who did not hide their emotions, were called witches. Men who reached a certain point of inner wisdom were called "Failed Sorcerers." Failed, because they were perceived as dangerous, and, therefore, 'evil'.

Even in literature, in the world of fiction, no one would read a book if the hero had no failings, or was not looking for redemption. Our Western intellectual traditions from Greece and Rome reinforce our failures. Our philosophical ancestors left us one over-riding message: that we don't know ourselves. Plato put this into the mouth of Socrates, and it is also said to have been carved onto the entrance to the oracle of Delphi: "Man, know yourself, and know that you are mortal!"

Similarly, our religious beliefs through Judaism and Christianity assure us that none of us live without sin. In the Christian environment, particularly, everyone is born a sinner.

Whether that belief or assumption is true or not, has recently met the test of scientific experimentation and measurement. We are not born 'sinners' in this scientific sense, but we are born with trauma. The part of our belief system that is true pertains to the often repeated Biblical phrase that the 'sins of the fathers are visited upon their sons for the third and fourth generation.' (paraphrased from Numbers 14:18)

Every parent who is not aware of his or her inner trauma, and the resulting fears and insecurities, will unconsciously pass those fears and insecurities right onto their precious children. I am a parent. I, in turn, will carry that trauma and unconsciously and habitually live through the causes of that trauma over and over again for the rest of my life. In the process, I pass on my trauma to my children.

Unless I heal myself! Or, if I cannot heal myself, then perhaps I can find a workable coping mechanism.

To make it even more poignant that I carry "the sins of the fathers to the third or fourth generation," scientific studies point directly at my genes that literally 'carry' the passed-on genes of my parents, grandparents and great-grandparents. Whatever physical problems they have suffered, they have passed on to me. I may not suffer them all, but the potential of their illnesses breaking out in me remains. Unless, of course, I choose to live in a different environment, create a different set of belief systems, and become slightly more aware of my life than they were. These environmental conditions that influence the genes are called 'epigenetics'.

Do I Need Healing?

Part 2: Then Start Breathing

I breathe slowly and deeply.
I breathe slowly and deeply for at least a minute—more if I am able.

I listen to my breath.

I listen to my breath to take my focus off the internal chatter, or ongoing analysis in my mind.

I join a yoga class and learn the various practices of pranayama (breathing).

It is the discipline of practice that heals, although it doesn't matter what I practice. My favorite is Kundalini Yoga, which I call the 'Yoga of endurance.' Because I was taught the 90-minute version of it, I only practice it once a week. During the week, on a daily basis, I prefer to do a 20-minute Qi-Gong practice. No matter what resistance I may have before the practice, when I am finished, there must be a surge of serotonin and oxytocin in my body because I feel good. I feel happy. It is not that I am healed permanently. There is no such thing. Life is a cycle.

Do I Need Healing?

Part 3: Three Ways to Recognize My Pain

Do I need healing? Yes, but only if I want to. For most of my life (and yes, the chances are for most of your life you have been doing this, too) I have avoided my emotional pain. Facing my pain creates a new coping cycle that works to bring awareness and lessen suffering.

For most of my life I have repressed my emotional pain. When it is repressed, the pain tends to break into my life in its various manifestations. I would break out in fits of anger; worry, anxiety, or insecurity. These 'normal' human activities, and others, such as wanting to be liked, or needing to help others at my own expense, are clear signs that I carry emotional pain.

For most of my life I have soothed my emotional pain. OK, so I did not use heroin or cocaine. I was too lazy to be a workaholic. But I was a French fries addict. I could not pass a fast-food outlet without ordering fries at least twice a day, and sometimes more often.

I was a sugar-addict. In Canada, the most popular coffee shop seems to be Tim Horton's. Their most popular coffee is a 'double-double' or a 'triple-triple'. I am talking about servings of cream and spoonfuls of sugar.

These are at least three ways to recognize that I have deeply held trauma within me:

1. Flying off the handle over and over again.
2. Having an addiction and denying it.
3. Chronically complaining, worrying and being afraid.

All three of these ways to recognize pain (and there are many others) tend to succumb to unconsciousness. As long as I am unconscious of how I behave, I cannot face my pain. I can't even admit that I have any. Reconnection, therefore, has to start with my becoming aware that I need to face my pain. I need to learn to cope with my repressed emotions.

Do I Need Healing?

Part 4: Three More Ways to Recognize My Pain

1. Being obsessive or compulsive.
2. Being xenophobic.
3. Being overly critical and judgmental.

Anyone can list another dozen signs that I carry pain. The ultimate arbiter of how many ways there are to recognize that I am a carrier of inner, emotional pain, is the number of recognized psychiatric disorders.

However, all of those disorders are symptoms. The cause, as Freud originally recognized it, is trauma. It is possible that Freud could not 'sell' childhood trauma to his patients, or his social circles. He hit upon sexual obsessions and caught everyone's interest and imagination.

But these were distractions.

Seeking Enlightenment

Part 1: Am I Ready?

I seek spiritual enlightenment and repress my emotions at the same time. How does that work?

If I carry a large load of repressed emotional baggage from my childhood, and I carry this load totally unconsciously, what are my chances at enlightenment?

This seeking of enlightenment while I am burdened with trauma has a built-in futility.

The ancient Greeks must have been aware of this problem, because of the way they had the Greek deities punish Sisyphus.

Sisyphus, although an ordinary mortal, was the founder and king of the city of Corinth. It is the same Corinth to whose Christian population, five hundred years or so later, Saint Paul wrote one of his epistles.

Sisyphus was not only a powerful king, he was also cunning. When he was fated to die, Hades himself came up from the underworld, with a pair of handcuffs, to make sure that this trickster of a king would be safely led down to his death. Handcuffs were, at that time, a recent invention. Sisyphus feigned such interest in how these cuffs worked that Hades was moved to demonstrate them—on himself. Before you knew it, Sisyphus had Hades immobilized in the handcuffs. It would have been funny, except that traffic into Hades came to a dead stop and, that interfered with the natural rhythms of life. People were not able to die!

Once Hades negotiated his release, Sisyphus was marched down to the Underworld, where he performed another trick, this time on Persephone, the Queen of the Underworld, and won himself a little more time to live. When all his tricks were used up, the Greek Gods enumerated his indiscretions and assigned him to roll a stone up a mountain, where it only would roll back down again, and tasked him to keep rolling it back up for all eternity.

Sisyphus' punishment was frustrating, pointless work. Whatever he did, undid itself. That is exactly what happens when I seek enlightenment but I am still driven by my unconscious pain and unresolved trauma! I reach the mountain-top and I slide right back down again. I have not actually dealt with my unresolved emotional pain, the foundation defect of my existence.

Seeking Enlightenment

Part 2: Comfort Inhibits Learning

Getting to know myself is a narrow path. Is it worth it?

Most of my life I was self-indulgent enough to not even try. My comfort zone was at stake! Trainers and Yoga teachers, however, have the key. Their advice is that I go into discomfort (though not into pain) so that my muscles and nerves, my proprioceptors, will learn.

Lewis Lapham, the American essayist, wrote a book called *Hotel America*. In that book he explored the comfort zone of our society in 1995. I wrote a poem that perfectly describes the concept:

Comfort Zone
(With apologies to Lewis Lapham)

Comfort Zone is the key concept
that drives the economy,
that drives moderate politics,
that allows small wars
in far corners of the world,
that makes us accept little famines
and big lies
and turns us blind to discomfort
in our own back yards.
Where is this Comfort Zone in North America?
It is hanging out of my trousers,
feeling good in my distended belly,
distended by comfort foods.
It is in my wallet,
comfortably stuffed with bills,
doled out by machines at every street corner,
at every convenience store and supermarket,
so that I don't have to be uncomfortable
facing a human teller when the account runs empty.
Comfort Zone is having two cars
and three bedrooms
and being able to get what I need
when I need it, whether I need it, or not.
Comfort Zone is knowing
that the depleted uranium bombs
with which we destroy the infrastructure
in Serbia or Afghanistan or Iraq
will not stop Apple iphones from being sold
in my local electronics shop.
Comfort Zone is believing
that nobody will invade
my private space without a warrant,
except, perhaps, for a hug.

It is the certainty that,
in case of a Stock Market crash,
my hedge funds will hold their value.
Comfort Zone is the satisfaction
that the Holiday Inn at Timbuktu
will serve catsup with my hamburger
and French Fries,
and that my insurance plan will pay
fifty thousand dollars
to replace my heart valves
in case I don't feel like changing
my eating habits.
Comfort Zone is an Anglican or United Church,
where nobody will ask me about Jesus,
whether I have him in my heart or in my pocket.
It is knowing that no matter
what kind of promises
politicians make during their campaigns,
it will make no difference to my lifestyle
whether or not they keep them, once elected.
Comfort Zone is knowing
that there are enough fanatics in Hotel America
that when pollution, inhumanity, poverty,
government encroachment,
big business arrogance or banking abuses
threaten my comfort level,
they will come out and march
and protest and speak up
and get pepper sprayed
and arrested and shot and thus,
keep my comfort level constant.
Comfort Zone is knowing you by a label,
which tells me all I want to know about you
and not having to listen
to all your petty theories
on human values, moral bankruptcy,

your patented stories
and vacuous conversations.
Comfort Zone is expecting that
when I say "Hello" to you
and ask you "How Are You?"
you know enough to stop after replying,
"I'm fine, and you?"
Published in *Slipped Out*, a poetry collection by Daniel Kolos (Pendas Productions, London, Ontario) 2003

Seeking Enlightenment

Part 3: What is 'Seeking'? What is 'Truth'?

Enlightenment, in one sense, is seeking truth.

Dr. Gabor Maté refers to A.H. Almaas who stresses that we have an innate drive for truth. But then, Dr. Maté notes that, although truth is liberating, we want it with strings or benefits attached. That doesn't work because truth comes unattached.

What is "Truth"? It seems that each of us has the potential of knowing our own truth within. In the New Testament, John 8: 32 states, "And ye shall know the truth, and the truth shall make you free." (KJV) Dr. Maté is fond of pointing out that it is not 'truth' that is liberating, but, rather, the knowledge of the truth!

"The experience of truth is much deeper than just an intellectual awareness. Very often, the truth is painful. All of our suffering comes from our attempts to avoid the truth... The more we want to avoid it (the truth about myself), the more we suffer. Given how painful truth can be sometimes, what does it take for people to open themselves to face it? Almaas, my teacher, says, "Only when compassion is present will people allow themselves to see the truth." That's why it is a compassionate inquiry." (Compassionate Inquiry certification course, Module 1, © 2018 Gabor Maté M. D. and Sat Dharam Kaur N. D., page 14. Quoted with permission.)

Let's examine what seeking is and what truth is, because like so many other words I have used, 'truth' and 'seeking' already carry a multitude of different meanings for so many people.

If I am 'seeking', the mere act could be an expression of deficiency. I am seeking enlightenment because I don't have it.

It can get worse! If I am seeking enlightenment in the service of having certainty, I am actually limiting myself. Certainty is a comfort and control issue, not a learning tool.

Unencumbered seeking is to follow the curiosity of the heart. Seeking is the pursuit for the intelligence of the heart!

If you have read Socrates, then you know that he took his students to the marketplace (agora) to ask where they could buy truth and beauty. Nobody was selling.

It seems that we each have our access to truth through our own hearts. A heart-driven search for one's truth might yield enlightenment. Heart-driven search for truth may be called 'spiritual'. Recent researchers, however, found that the heart has duplicated several brain functions and acts as the 'intelligence' for our non-intellectual and non-analytical processes. We have our intellect, we have our body, and to complete the checks and balances, we have our heart. The heart, it seems, is able to guide the other two with its unwavering love and intelligence. Joseph Chilton Pearce wrote a delightful book, packed with scientific research on the vital role of our heart in guiding us to our truth called *The Biology of Transcendence.*

If I am on a spiritual journey to enlightenment, but avoid truth on the spiritual level, John Wellwood has coined the phrase for this shortcoming: "Spiritual Bypass." Spiritual bypass has side-effects! By not honoring the interplay, but practicing emotional avoidance, according to Dr. Maté, "... we detach/disable our immune system and open ourselves up to disease."

The tripartite human system—body, mind, and heart (as the seat of our emotions)—influence and act upon each other constantly throughout our lives. Any spiritual seeker who leaves one or two aspects of this system of checks and balances out of the equation will likely increase his/her suffering.

OK, so the Buddha said, "Life is suffering." But the current 'mindfulness' movement claims correctly, that "When you are in the moment, there is no pain." The Buddha likely knew that!

CHAPTER

85

Seeking Enlightenment

Part 4: What Gets in the Way?

If I am a spiritual seeker, does that mean I am no longer supposed to express my anger? Not so. When someone crosses my boundary without my permission, anger is a perfectly appropriate response!

Whereas there is room for anger, there is no room for fear on the path to enlightenment. The Buddha demonstrated this fearlessness when the king of the demons lined up his entire army against him and demanded battle. The Buddha said, "You are an illusion. I have no fear. Do your worst." The demons were helpless. They depend on our fears for their power.

I have been using the words 'emotional' and 'spiritual' interchangeably. It is necessary to know that if my development is only on the spiritual level, then I am restricting/limiting myself. Not only do I have three levels within me; the intellectual, the physical and the emotional/spiritual, but I constantly interact with the outside world on several more levels, such as the physiological, emotional, social, and cultural.

All these levels work together. A limitation in any one of these levels affects all the others. For example, religious belief without faith is empty. For religious belief to be fruitful, it requires a practice and a sense of joy.

Seeking Enlightenment

Part 5: What About Addiction?

Addictions effect brain physiology. Let's see how they get in the way of my enlightenment. Addictions, according to Dr. Gabor Maté, "arise from dislocation from family, land, home. Drinking was known even in the ancient world, drunkenness was a cult, but addiction was not on the broad scale we have in industrial times."

His view is that ceremonial use of a substance is in service of seeking cultural connections. Addiction is about separation. When we are using substances for ceremonial purposes, we are essentially looking for ourselves.

One form of addiction is to dwell on the past. What happened to me thirty, forty or fifty years ago can completely occupy my mind, and interfere with my daily relationships. If I keep interpreting my past rather than letting it go, it also interferes with my search for enlightenment.

How can I free my mind from the past? I can let go, not react, and not interpret the past as I used to.

A friend from the upper west side of Manhattan was knocked down onto the sidewalk by a bicycle three years ago. It was a terrible accident that broke her teeth, her nose, and traumatized her. Her healing has been very, very slow. One of the attitudes that has slowed her healing is her conviction that it will happen again. She will take her dog and walk on side streets, but assiduously avoids Broadway, which has much pedestrian and bicycle activity. We have been friends for decades. Every time we speak, either on the telephone or in person, she veers into this most recent trauma. She cannot get past it.

Recovery from addiction is also finding something we have lost. If we have lost something, we had it in the first place. Recovery is a euphemism for reconnection. It is, therefore, part of the path to enlightenment!

Seeking Enlightenment

Part 6: Reinventing the Wheel

Skeptics insist that there is nothing new under the sun. They claim that we keep recycling the same experiences generation after generation and learning the same lessons as people have done for millennia. The only thing that changes, they claim, is the technology.

That perspective, of course, is perfectly valid. However, it is just one perspective of many I can hold.

My current perspective is that each one of us has to learn and experience those same ancient truths/cycles within ourselves in order to become complete human beings. In my opinion, I have to reinvent the wheel. That is, I have to have *my* experience. Your experience may teach me a thing or two, but I have to have my own before the lesson becomes personalized and meaningful to me on all three levels: intellectually, physically and emotionally.

I have to intuit, on my own, what my truth is. The fact that millions of people have already intuited the same truth does not help me.

Gurucharan Khalsa, a former student of Yogi Bhajan and today a 'Guru' in his own right, has developed a program and written a book called *21 Stages of Meditation*. Stage 2 is "Boredom"!

Gurucharan delights to see his students raise their eyebrows when they learn that boredom is actually a useful component of our physiology. It is a necessary and integral part of the cycle of creativity. There is nothing in our arsenal of feelings, thoughts and experiences that is useless. However, all of these need coordination, and that takes awareness!

Seeking Enlightenment

Part 7: Is Being Pissed Off the Key to Enlightenment?

Where do I seek discomfort in order to learn?

I don't need to seek it. Discomfort comes to me.

All I have to do is get pissed off. It is a form of discomfort.

The trick is, that instead of mouthing off at the person who pissed me off, I keep in mind that being pissed off is my learning opportunity. The one who pissed me off provided the trigger and has nothing more to do with it. In the full context of a healthy connection, I should thank the person who triggered me!

In the anatomy of discomfort, someone has just connected me with my pain. If I consider that people pay thousands of dollars to go to psychotherapists to be connected to their pain, consider the benefits of being pissed off! This interaction offers me the opportunity to face my pain, accept it, release it and be a step closer to enlightenment. I can't say it often enough that I should hug and thank the one who pissed me off.

My next step has to be the pain itself. Dr. Maté might ask me to hold that pain a moment longer. When I stay with the pain, I find a memory, and it is usually a childhood memory. Dr. Maté emphasizes that, although the memory is from the past, the pain itself, though, is here, now. That's why it hurts!

While it feels 'current', that pain has been there since my early childhood. It came from a time when I desperately needed something—often, nothing more than a hug. My mother was busy and I became angry. Or I wanted to be held before supper and mother was busy cooking. Father was reading. I was angry, frustrated, and perhaps even wanted revenge. I may have even decided, "I am not going to eat my supper." Whatever happened, I did not get what I wanted, I was not heard, I was ignored, and worst of all, I interpreted the situation as not being loved.

So when you piss me off, all this childhood rage floods my emotional circuits and I want revenge.

If I lash out at you, am I going to get what I wanted as a child by making you feel bad? NO! If I am totally unconscious of my feelings, I can rage. It might make *you* feel bad, but it will not make *me* feel happy. The better choice is to remain aware of my pain, become aware of how it arose in the first place, and accept the fact that, as a child, I didn't get what I wanted. That may be all I need. This sort of acceptance is the first building-block of a successful coping strategy!

Such unfulfilled needs were many in childhood. Each required me to devise ways to try to get what I wanted, and these manipulations developed my personality. I developed my personality at a cost. I lost connection with my emotional development. The trauma that was suppressed is the trauma of separation from a vital component of my own life: my own authenticity.

Not getting what I wanted was just another trigger. As an adult I often still don't get what I want, but I have learned coping mechanisms, and can live with the resulting frustration or anger.   To compensate for the disconnection from my own authenticity, or my 'soul', I have to embark on a search to reconnect.

So here I am, searching how to reconnect to my soul, because viewing the world through the lens of my own authenticity is the beginning of enlightenment.

CHAPTER

89

Connecting with Your Child

Part 1: What's the Problem with My Daughter?

Did you ever yell at your daughter and remember that it was the same way that your mother yelled at you when you were a little girl? Every time my mother yelled at me, it was always my fault! Or, was it?

I am slightly over my head here, because I am male and I don't have a daughter. But I have heard enough interviews with mothers of all ages to have grasped, at least intellectually, and perhaps compassionately, the process that develops between mothers and their daughters. In the end, this process is not that much different than what happens between fathers and sons.

As a parent, you have likely forgotten that when you were your daughter's age, you didn't know any better either.

So why does a little girl (or boy, for that matter) not behave the way her mother expects her to behave? Why is she not acting responsibly?

Let's just look at two reasons out of the hundreds of possibilities. One may be that you, as the mother (or father) are telling your little girl what you expect, but you are not role modeling it.

Children learn mimetically. They will mimic you, ape you, and even make fun of how you behave. In the process, they begin to behave like you do. If that is not how you want your little girl (or boy) to behave, modeling one behavior, and telling her to do something else will simply not work.

Another possibility is that no matter how hard your daughter tries to be responsible and behave like you ask her to, her frontal lobe has not yet developed enough to grasp this. This physiological vacuum is most evident in the teenage years. Those years are also the time when the hapless parents expect more and more responsibility from their children.

Don't panic! There is hope. There is such a thing as learned responsibility, or, rather, a learned response. Pavlov demonstrated that with dogs. That was a hundred years or so ago. Today, dogs are trained even to smell the presence of cancer in people! And every one of us who are parents, cajole, threaten and reward our children for behaving in certain ways. Sometimes our children will do as we expect.

Reward, therefore, is a most effective program. If I reward my child time and again, I will likely get a responsible behavior. What reward to use? Not candy!

What children don't receive enough of is genuine communication from their parents. I can tell my child "I love you!" over and over again, and say nothing else meaningful. That is good, but it is not enough!

The response my child needs is a heartfelt hug, and a meaningful conversation—an inclusive and ongoing relationship. When my child speaks, I have to practice compassionate listening. My response must make sure that my child is 'heard'. Not only will that child 'behave' responsibly, that child will also be emotionally healthy because a safe connection with a parent (or two, if possible) is the foundation of reconnection with one's self.

OK, so establishing a meaningful, inclusive and loving relationship with my child is not exactly a 'reward' in the Pavlovian sense. You, as the parent, can do something about it, not the child. There is no fault. There is no responsibility. There is only that inclusive, aware relationship.

Connecting with Your Child

Part 2: I Am the Problem!

Between Pavlovian training and role modeling, the latter wins hands down. It is a matter of control versus the natural, organic development of the child, together with a steadfast, supportive, inclusive and loving relationship with whichever caregiver is available. Yes, I might be able to train my child to behave responsibly on the outside, but what I actually taught my child was to control his/her life, and possibly, repress spontaneity on the inside.

Many mothers come to their wits' end worrying about their child. The worry, the anxiety, and the guilt, gets out of proportion for her. The old Tibetan adage which states that if I don't deal with my pain it becomes worse, hits every one of us!

"I've done everything I could to make your life easier," a mother would insist to her teenager, "so why won't you talk to me?" In fact, what the mother has taught her daughter is the worry, the anxiety, and the guilt that has been gnawing at her insides throughout her child's life. And it is the same worry, anxiety and guilt that the mother grew up with, and the mother's mother grew up with. No one has ever taken the responsibility to upgrade their own, inner, emotional issues until recently. The practice of releasing unresolved trauma is less than twenty years old! Compassionate Inquiry has only been publicly demonstrated since 2014!

It is me, the parent, who has a problem, not the child. If I notice that my worry, anxiety, and guilt become worse and worse each year, it is time to give myself some self-care. I have done most of my influencing of my child before s/he is two. If I want to continue my influence, it is because my insecurities have been left untreated, and all I can do is to build defenses and try to control my own, and my child's, environment.

Remaining in control is hard work. In his book, *When the Body Says No!* Dr. Gabor Maté systematically demonstrates how our bodies respond to emotions that don't nourish us, but to which we helplessly cling most of our lives.

Connecting with Your Child

Part 3: Reconnecting

What happens when you don't get through to your child and lose him or her? Can you reconnect?

This question is a nightmare scenario. Parents, no matter what economic strata of our society they come from, regularly lose emotional contact with their children. Young teenagers run away from home, turn to drugs, join gangs and do worse and worse things that the parent has no control over.

Some parents simply disown their children. They are content never to see them again, and never to have to deal with them again. It may be tough love. It may be sheer cold-heartedness. It may be a hundred other things.

One single mother in my neck of the woods 'lost' her fourteen-year-old son. It didn't look that bad on the surface. He still lived at home and went to school. He still showed up at the school bus each morning. At home, however, he was sullen and never spoke.

If his mother pushed him, questioned him, or accused him, at some point, he would yell back at her. Pushing a frightened boy into a corner is like pushing a frightened tiger into the corner. You leave them no room but to attack you. If you are out hunting, that is exactly what you want: to have your prey cornered.

But if the frightened being is your own son, and each time you corner him he either blows up at you or speaks to you less and less, healing is not going to happen. Remember that for a cornered child, even a teenager, there are only three survival responses: fight, flight, or freeze.

This particular single mother began to read about what her options were. She decided that calling the police or Children's Aid was out of the question and so were psychiatric intervention and pharma drugs. She made her choice. She decided to reconnect with her son. She arranged her work so she would begin at 9:30 in the morning and quit at 2:30 in the afternoon. She was fortunate that she could. With her savings, her income was adequate to run her household for at least two years.

She started taking her son to school in her vehicle. For the first three or four months, not a word was spoken between them on these rides. She persevered. Then, the boy said something. The mother acknowledged what her son had said, and then she shut up.

In the following weeks, the boy began to talk more and more. The mother listened, and did not interrupt. She may or may not have known that by doing so, she was creating a safe place for her son. Chances are she knew, because she had read books and articles while she was looking for help. She had created an environment in which verbal sharing could be renewed. She created an environment in which her son believed he was heard!

By the time school was over, they were having conversations both in the vehicle and at home. In most cases, teenage children will tend to gather with their peer group and take their 'advice', but this mother knew that at least her son could talk with her, and their closeness was renewed.

One of these books may have been, *Hold On to Your Kids-Why Parents Need to Matter More Than Peers* that came out in 2004, coauthored by Gordon Neufeld and Gabor Maté.

Responsible Self-care

Part 1: Am I Responsible for What I Think About Myself, or For the Way I think About Myself?

ell no! Well … maybe. What's in it for me?

What are our responsibilities?

"Our primary responsibility is to our spiritual identity, followed by responsibilities to our wellbeing, our family and friends, our jobs, the planet and future generations. When we are responsible to something, we respond to its needs. If this is something other than our ego, something with a higher purpose that entails loving sacrifice, we often receive assistance through the flow of the universal energy" (page 418, *Beyond Addiction* workbook, ©Sat Dharam Kaur, N.D. Jan. 2018)

How do I show or exercise responsibility for my "spiritual identity?"

First, I have to acknowledge that I am a composite of body, mind and soul. I am a physical being with physical needs. I am an intellectual/ imaginative being with ideas and dreams, and an emotional creature whose feelings most likely have been hurt and shut down in childhood, and has a need to reconnect to those feelings.

There is a good chance that in my twenties and thirties I did not know who I was, other than my name and address, and perhaps my accomplishments to that point. The way I identified myself was as a composite of what people thought of me. Once, I visited a former U. S. Army buddy in New York City. He was a conscious objector who had spent his tour of duty as a supply clerk in a training center. Upon seeing how I responded to the hustle and bustle of that large city, he said, "Daniel, you are so neurotic." As a result, "neurotic" was like a badge of honor, and I accepted it as a label. I enjoyed life, I was sensually alive, I worried about a lot of things and disliked many things. If that meant 'neurotic', well, so be it! I had no idea that I was unconscious (or ignorant) of a large part of my own life! Neither did my friend.

Just as I accepted other people's decisions about what I would do for the first 24 years of my life, I accepted other people's assessment of who I was. I took no responsibility for who I was. Chances are that now, after years of philosophical, spiritual and more recently psychological studies, I have amassed a plethora of labels about who I am. However, once I dispense with the labels and degrees and honors, I very likely don't know myself at all. After all, I keep finding surprisingly repressed emotional pockets within me all the time!

I have exercised no responsibility for what or how I think of myself for most of my life. In short, I have remained unconscious. In the classic psychotherapeutic sense, I have lived from one ego-satisfaction to the next and let the glory—or the failure—define me.

Responsible Self-Care

Part 2: What is Self-Care?

If I am a composite of body, mind and soul, and each one of these has its own special needs, then I have to find ways to fulfill those needs! I have to make room for the ideas and dreams, and deal with the hurt feelings of the child who still controls, albeit unconsciously, my interactions with other people. The repressed fear of that child within me unconsciously holds me back from interacting, or even re-opening a connection with my emotional development.

When I make a mistake, it is that hurt child within me that feels ashamed. As an adult, I can give myself permission to make mistakes. I can correct them.

When someone insults me, it is the child within me that feels hurt. As an adult, having experienced "mindfulness" courses, I know that whoever insulted me, was speaking from his/her own pain-unconsciously. I have to get to know myself in order to reach that hurt child I was in my youth!

Let's take self-care for the body as an example. What I eat, how I eat it, how I breathe, how much I exercise, how much I sleep, what yoga practice or discipline I am committed to, how much massage therapy I get (the list can go on and on) all define my commitment to self-care of my body.

Although the mind and body are interconnected, the mind or the intellect, requires care as well. I first heard of the body-mind connection when I read that Chess Master Bobby Fisher ran a few miles before every chess game. Really? Yes! So my exercise regimen is self-care both for the body and the mind. That connection has been scientifically researched and settled. However, having a good conversation or two each day, reading a book, writing a journal entry, a poem or a story, are all primary care for the mind!

The real challenge here, at least for me, was how to practice self-care for my emotional self? I had no idea. I was taught, most likely mimetically, not to show my emotions. When someone asked me "How do you feel?" my answer was an inevitable "Great, thanks!" I would not have been able to identify a feeling within myself if I tried. In fact, as I am developing an authentic relationship with my environment, my greatest challenge is how to answer that question: "How are you?"

One recurring answer should be, "I'm afraid, thanks!"

I grew up with a fear of authority figures, beginning with my father and my elementary school teachers. Their generation followed the German-Hungarian strictest possible discipline with the severest possible punishments. That has always been one fear that I could identify in myself.

I was in graduate school at age 29-32 when I realized that I could not speak to one particular professor without going into panic mode. My throat closed up because my heart had risen to 150 beats-per-minute. My hands would shake, and I would sometimes forget what I came to say or hand in. He was amused, so that was no help. After three or four embarrassing episodes like that over two years during which I tried to avoid visiting him by myself in his office, I decided to get over it. I forced myself to visit him at least once each week, stumbled through my questions, sometimes writing them down ahead of time on a slip of paper, until my body calmed down, my voice became normal, my mind cleared. That was my second consciously conceived, planned and executed act of self-care up to that point in my life.

CHAPTER

94

Responsible Self-Care

Part 3: Resistance to Commitment

I have first-hand experience resisting commitment. Perhaps I was afraid of responsibility and the shame and uncomfortable feelings that come with failure, should I not be able to stick to a commitment. Perhaps I had not yet developed the self-esteem to succeed. Or I lacked the energy, inspiration and motivation to press forward to the next level. It may have been all of the above!

This is what happened. I entered the Beyond Addiction Program: the Yogic Way of Recovery, in 2015. This program partners with Kundalini Yoga and during the nine-day intensive I could only do about fifteen percent of the yoga exercises. For the next four months of the course I operated only on the intellectual level, reading the lessons of the Program, and avoiding the yoga exercises. I had a resistance to yoga, and I was not even aware of it!

Soon after the actual four-month course ended, I linked up with a 'study-buddy' from Massachusetts, who was really keen on doing Kundalini

Yoga. We practiced via Zoom, a video app. Her sheer enthusiasm carried me, together with my reluctance, for the next eight months. Somewhere along that timeline I realized that the 'head' knowledge I had acquired was not enough. After each yoga exercise, when we sat quietly to find our body sensations, I felt nothing.

I decided to return for a second round of the entire training. That was a commitment. I found that after a year of reluctantly doing Kundalini Yoga once a week, I could do more than seventy-five percent of the exercises during the nine-day intensive! I was ecstatic! I almost called myself "Daniel Yogi" but kept it to myself.

In my enthusiasm, though, I found two more study-buddies online and proposed that we embark on a sixteen month practice, during which we would devote an entire month to each of the sixteen Beyond Addiction lessons. It was at that point that my first study-buddy said, "I cannot make such a long-term commitment."

I was flabbergasted, and may even have felt disappointed, except that I still had trouble connecting with even the simplest feelings in my body. The only thing I can admit to, is that I likely became attached to my first study-buddy, grew rather fond of her and missed her when she withdrew from the Kundalini Yoga practice. I encouraged her to begin with our expanded group, and if it proved to be too much, that she could stop it any time. That decision to resist such a long commitment must have been made with a deep-set, unconscious fear, because my first Yoga partner literally disappeared from my life.

Within myself, however, I no longer recognized myself and my previous, lifetime's worth of avoiding commitment. It was my turn to be enthusiastic and carry the other practitioners with me for the first few weeks. Then, we began to carry each other. They were both committed! We practiced Kundalini Yoga each morning for ninety minutes. It was long enough to let me tune into my body and identify feelings, especially uncomfortable ones, and to begin dealing with them.

It was important for me to recognize my resistance to commitment and explore the root of it so that I could better understand it. The training itself offered a particular exercise. It was this: to make a list of what I might gain by resisting commitment, and what I might lose if I didn't commit.

Responsible Self-Care

Part 4: What Do I Gain and Lose by Resisting Commitment?

What Do I Gain by Resisting?

1. More time to do other things, which usually end up being distractions.
2. A sense of freedom, which may be an illusion because boredom soon follows.
3. A sense of pride that I don't need others, and that I am my own 'man'!

What Do I Lose?

1. A sense of purpose—that I am doing something meaningful, and self-promoting.
2. The fear that I may be missing out on something important for me, because there is still more to learn.

3. A chance to integrate my body-mind-emotional responses with others, because it seems that in a group setting, each of us is empowered far more than we would be if we practiced alone.

This phenomenon may be associated with the adage that "the whole is greater than the sum of its parts." This group-integration or enhancement appears also in the words of Jesus when he is quoted as saying, "Where two or three are gathered in my name, there I am also."

The Holy Grail of Spiritual Pursuit

I believe I have come around in circles several times by now, hopefully in ever tightening spirals to show that the Holy Grail of spiritual/emotional pursuits, even the seeking of enlightenment, is the emotional reconnection to one's own Soul.

There is nothing new about this conclusion. Eastern teachings often use this imagery and tell the story of a seeker who is guided to find what he needs at the top of a very treacherous mountain, but it's worth the climb. So the seeker goes, endures great hardships, goes through great dangers and reaches the mountaintop. There, in a well-protected cave, he finds a thick book, and he opens it to begin the teachings that he has been looking for.

There is nothing written in this book. It is a book of empty pages! Or, in variant stories, he opens the book to find only a mirror. What he has been looking for all along is his own Self.

Intuition

Part 1: Intuitional/Rational Balance

Call it intuition, call it a hunch, but each of us has these "inner knowings" or gut feelings from time to time. Some people have an abundance of intuition. I met one such friend who confidently told me that she does not need to know anything from a book or a teacher. All she needs to know comes to her from the "Universe" when she needs it. After years of working at a Michigan conference, she left for Sedona and is still working there, dispensing universal knowledge.

I have to admit that I have not reached that point within myself. In fact, having come from the other end of the scale—a complete reliance on my intellectual faculties—I will be deeply satisfied to reach a working balance where I can rely on my intuition and have my intellect as a back-up. I may no longer believe that by the time my next book is finished, but, for now, this is my truth. The next book, by the way, will carry the title, *Responsible? Well..., Maybe...*

Intuition is a natural human tool. It is available to everyone. It is like thinking, but only in the sense that intuition has to be trained. We spend eight years in school in order to train our intellect. We learn to read, write and solve mathematical functions. We spend another four years in high school, and lots of people go on to earn a B.A., an M.A. or a Ph.D.

All of these public and higher educational efforts develop our rational mind, our intellect, and our ability to analyze and solve problems. I might say that rational/intellectual learning stems from our cultural presupposition that life is a series of problems to be solved. This perspective is a perfectly acceptable model that usually works. After all, every toddler is filled with an unexplainable urge to overcome obstacles!

However, the rational functions don't work

When emotions are high.

When emotions are repressed.

When the rational mind is short-circuited by prescription drugs.

When the rational mind is short-circuited by alcohol and hallucinogens.

Even at the best of times, our senses and perceptions are so different that our entire system of rational and objective interpretation of reality varies from one person to another like night and day.

We need to develop both our intuition and our rational mind to the point where these will benefit one another.

Intuition

Part 2: How Do I Develop Intuition?

Back in the early nineteen-seventies I signed up for and began to receive mail-order lessons from The Rosicrucians. Founded and originally run by an advertising executive, the modern 'mystical order' knew how to advertise. One of the first experiments I remember from this time is picking up envelopes the post office had delivered and placing them on my forehead with my eyes closed and trying to guess who had sent it. I was zero for a hundred the very first year.

Why? Because by 1970 I'd had sixteen years of rational/intellectual education. I needed to catch up, on my intuitive education so I began to 'guess' outcomes, including horse races. I participated in penny-flipping, to see if I could guess, or even influence whether a penny would land on heads or tails. My efforts were inconclusive, but my reward was that I was not the only one experimenting. At Princeton University similar experiments were being conducted with statistically significant results.

The simple intent that I wanted to develop my intuition beyond the occasional hunch slowly let more and more of these hunches through. In order to further my learning, I read many spiritual non-fiction authors. In that process, I found that I tended to prefer those with a scientific background.

Joseph Chilton Pearce wrote a series of books, beginning with *A Crack in the Cosmic Egg*, and I lapped up his research. When Lynn MacTaggart came out with *The Field*, I was in science heaven. However, it was Bruce Lipton, the Biologist and Gregg Braden the Geologist who helped me set my intuition aflame.

Lipton's book, *The Biology of Belief*, showed me that as a collection of a hundred (or three hundred) trillion living cells, a collective trust exists that my 'consciousness' will pick up the signals of what is best for this phenomenally large number of 'individual entities' to survive. These are not his words, but my own take-away.

CHAPTER 99

Intuition

Part 3: Role of the Body and the Unconscious in Developing Intuition

The possibility that intuition may be my body 'speaking' to me was exciting. I began to ask my body questions. Within a day, or after a good night's sleep, I 'knew' the answers. Bruce Lipton also mused whether this totality of our cellular consciousness may comprise what our religious predecessors called our "Soul."

Gregg Braden wrote a book on what intentions do for us and our 'knowing'. His audio book, *Spontaneous Healing of Belief*, spelled out, chapter by chapter that we, as human beings, have a powerful connection to our inner self. The Swiss Psychoanalyst, Carl Gustav Jung, noted that among the many Archetypes we human beings carry within ourselves, one is the Capital S "Self".

This Self may bring us closest to a sense of divinity. Why? Because as we begin to sense our non-verbal connectedness to our cellular bodies, a sense of wellbeing, even sacredness, fills our consciousness.

Jung, however, had more to say on this matter. For thirteen years I attended a monthly Jungian dream analysis workshop with the New York Psychoanalyst, Rosemary Gosselin who had relocated to my neighborhood. Jung noted that the unconscious mind, though it may absorb everything, communicates through symbols and dreams.

First, I noted for myself, that, just as there is the hippocampus that separates the functions of the rational brain from the functions of the limbic brain, there is also a barrier between what we conceive as the conscious and the unconscious mind. In his monumental book, *The Act of Creation,* Arthur Koestler concluded that it was only after the rational mind had been completely exhausted of all possibilities that the unconscious, or creative mind kicks in and solves the problem.

Intuition is most likely a function of our unconscious mind. Access to our intuition, similar to our access to 'the sacred' does not happen on command. It happens in its own time and space. It happens when we are in a 'receptive' state of mind. It happens during meditation, whether on a studio mat or on a walk through the woods, or listening to the surf on a deserted beach.

We can develop intuition while gardening or even washing dishes. It is the act of listening to our body. I figure that if my consciousness is the sum total of the individual consciousness of each of my cells, then listening to my 'gut feelings' is the best way for me to access my intuition.

Intuition

Part 4: Can Intuition Be "Soul-Guidance"?

When I was young, I 'accepted' Jesus Christ as my personal Savior. I had no idea what I was doing, but it felt right. When it came to choosing a Bible verse that best described my relationship to God, I chose Psalm 25, verses 4 and 5:

"Show me thy ways, O Lord; teach me thy paths.

[5] Lead me in thy truth, and teach me: for thou art the God of my salvation; on thee do I wait all the day." (King James Version)

As a teenager, I didn't get that I was a "sinner", but I had "bad" thoughts and self-harming habits, so I thought I qualified. I didn't get "Salvation" either, but I liked the idea that somehow Jesus would live in my heart 'from now on.'

Later in life I began meditating. I found that there is a 'sacred' feeling inside me when I am all here, breathing deeply, and empty of fears and worries. I equated that feeling with the divinity of Jesus having entered my heart. I also realized that, at the age of 16, I intuitively exercised a 'spiritual' yearning that, as Pearce had pointed out in his third book, *The Magical Child,* is a natural part of childhood brain development.

Intuition

Part 5: The Conundrum of Certainty and Uncertainty

Having come from long years of intellectual training, my first question was, 'when do I need my Soul's guidance?'

OK, I may be slow, but eventually I realized that my plans did not always work out. I decided that I could use Soul-guidance most of the time, if not all the time.

My next question was "How can I connect with my Soul's guidance more and more often?" At my very first business coaching session in 2013, I came to understand that listening to my intuition is a matter of trust.

I created a simple formula for myself. If I accept and view myself as a tripartite being with an interactive body-mind-emotional system, then I will attract the right guidance most of the time, and perhaps even all of the time.

I began journaling three different times. Each time I had written about my life. The first time I journaled about my life path with the Rosicrucians. The second time I did it as part of my Anthroposophic studies. The third time it was with the Beyond Addiction Program.   When I reviewed these journals, I had a surprise! I had been "Soul-guided" all my life, but did not know it! My Soul-guidance was, perhaps, a survival response to my ignorance, cluelessness and helplessness.

Now that I have started to think, analyze, introspect, meditate and practice, all I have to do is trust. There are no formulas and no expectations. Just trust, because the system has been working in spite of 'me'.

Nevertheless, a conundrum arose for me immediately. On the one hand, there is no certainty when it comes to Soul guidance. I never know what happens next. On the other hand, my habituated mind craves certainty.

When I first watched a Tony Robbins video, he listed his version of the six basic human needs. These included certainty as well as uncertainty. I roared with laughter and approval. My conundrum seemed to be universal.

The process or interplay between certainty and uncertainty is never ending. It is like riding the surf. All the waves are different. There are little ones and there are big ones. Surfers are patient enough to wait for the "Big One." I decided that I must become a Soul-guidance surfer.

Intuition

Part 6: Confident in My Unconscious?

A Poem

1.
Easily donned, quickly undone
Certainty turns into uncertainty

2.
I want to be mindful and aware
to exert control over my life
but ninety percent of my actions
are habituated and unconscious!

3.
Teachers jump into the gap.
"Reprogram your Subconscious,
use your tools: your will and intent,
to create a confident Unconscious.

"Take stock of your hopes and dreams,
choose your talents and abilities
and you will have your customized curriculum
of a confidence-boosting practicum."

4.
Easily learned, quickly forgotten,
uncertainty must become a way of life.

Self Correction

Part 1: How I Responded to a Toxic Situation

I always have a choice to do more than the three survival tools allow me to do. As a self-aware adult, I can, but I don't have to fight, I don't have to run away, and I don't have to hide from most situations.

I have the choice to accept the situation, make peace within me, and then move on. Even in such a worst-case event as a rape, a home robbery or a public humiliation, I have the choice to accept the fact that it happened, process the pain and take my life back. Nobody can take the experience away from me! But it is my choice whether or not to process it, accept it, grieve it and move on.

Or not. I can nurse a wound throughout a lifetime, or let my experience become a principle, and a foundation for everything else I do. Margaret Fulton, originally an English professor at Wilfred Laurier University, for example, lost her fiancé early in World War II. She decided to honor him by not seeking someone else to be with. She lived a rich, rewarding life becoming the president of several universities over her career and traveling abroad teaching and inspiring highly placed women from all over the world. Her way of honoring her fallen lover spilled over into all her activities, so that everyone she met felt honored.

In order to move forward in life, I had to accept the fact that my father beat me, or just slapped me in the face as his first reaction to whatever I may have done. He shouted at me in great anger, and told me that I was stupid and/or incompetent. Curiously, this treatment only started when I was in the third grade. Until then I was a straight A student. When the beatings started, my grades dropped, until by seventh grade, I was failing two subjects.

It was only decades later I found out that my father was suffering from several major traumas. First, of course, was the probable PTSD he was exposed to during World War II. Second, when I was 8, he was accused of causing great damage at a factory-wing which he directed, and he was jailed. Even though the charges were false and he was freed, the Hungarian Communist system would not allow him to work after he had been jailed. Since the Communist government was the only legal employer in Hungary, my father was out of a job for life. It was a shock to his emotional system that he could not handle, and reinforced his previous traumas. His way of soothing the pain was to punish and belittle everyone around him. When he did that to me, he was successful in transferring much of his repressed emotions into me. That is what children do best: pick up the emotions of their parents.

But when my father exploded in ager at his own friends, or my mother and her friends, then there were shouting matches and a few adult slaps-in-the-face from those not afraid of my father. None of these incidents solved anything. His emotional outbursts continued.

When I was 12 and the Hungarian Revolution broke out, my mother left him, taking me and my younger sister to the United States.

My father did not have a chance at processing his pain and 'self-correction' by accepting what had happened to him. But I had a chance to accept him for what he was and not carry my childhood hatred and fear of him with me. Long before I learned about emotional trauma, my friends 'held' me in their compassion. They allowed me to tell my story, and helped me change my perspective from that of a hapless victim to one of a sovereign being. I could still be stupid and incompetent at times, but eventually developed the self-confidence and self-love to take each day and make it the best day of my life.

OK, so I was able to overcome a few of those emotions, but not all of them. I continued to carry with me my belief that "I am not good enough." I knew that I was not an 'idiot', but the subtleties of beliefs about 'being useless' or 'unable to succeed' remained with me till recently. These are beliefs that I may have passed on to my oldest son. In spite of my best efforts not to treat him like my father treated me, I nevertheless instilled in him a doubt about his own competence and ability to succeed. I did not know that children pick up their parents' greatest worries and secret fears until I embarked on the Compassionate Inquiry certification program.

Self Correction

Part 2: Wherever You are, Make Peace

A brilliant woman, boss of a busy industrial complex, started studying to become an addiction counselor. I will call her Alfreda, although that is not her real name. After twenty years of a successful career, she began to find the working environment toxic. The closer she found herself to her counseling degree and the attendant practicum, the more toxic her workplace became to her.

She was deeply afraid of leaving her position. It was a secure source of income and she feared financial instability. She was well aware that working with private clients could have drawbacks: that they often don't show up; that even when her addiction counseling business would take off, the income would be uncertain for a few years.

In an addiction counseling 'practice session' one weekend, Alfreda had a client who mirrored her anxieties. In a single moment of insight, she could see that her body had been responding to her toxic work environment with an ever-worsening set of physical symptoms. She had to excuse herself before the client to take a few minutes to process her realization. She noted that the closer she came to her certification, the more she experienced emotional upheavals and the sicker she felt.

By the time Alfreda completed her degree and received her certification, her triumph was practically squelched. She had not yet left her workplace! She could hardly function and had to go to a therapist. It took her only one visit to realize that she must leave her 'job'. Becoming a certified addiction counselor was a dream-come-true, but every day that she delayed leaving her job made her feel worse and worse.

She contemplated her fear and wondered if she needed to reach some 'bottom' before she would act. Her whole body shook when she handed in her resignation at work. But even at that point, she had given herself what she was hoping to be a financial cushion of three months to disengage.

Alfreda returned to her own psychotherapist and realized that she had created her own conundrum. It was not the workplace that was becoming more and more toxic. It was her own internal struggle with trusting her choice of career change that had upset her. It was the fear of the unknown that had ravaged both her emotions and her body. Those three months became not merely the financial cushion she was hoping for, but also a time to heal. By the time she left her corporation, she held no grudges, and was ready to embark on her dream.

In his book, "When the Body Says NO!" Dr. Gabor Maté shows example after example from his own private medical practice, as well as from published biographies and large-scale research studies that any and all internal, body-born-diseases may be influenced by stress.

The physical body its emotional component form a powerful bond that can influence both our lives within, as well as the world outside.

Self Correction

Part 3: From Blame to Responsibility

Trusting my inner guidance is challenging. This trust, however, develops with practice. It helps when I stop blaming things on others. It helps if I stop worrying about whose fault it is.

Blaming my problems on others has never actually solved one. In fact, 'blaming' looks more and more like an addiction: I cannot stop doing it; it seems to soothe my pain, but doesn't take that pain away; it may be harmful to the people I blame, and it severely harms my relationships with them.

Blame can also have a larger, cultural enactment. It is often called 'scapegoating', a form of collective persecution that Rene Gerard, the French philosopher, studied and wrote about. When a large portion of the population refuses to accept responsibility, they experience what Thomas Hübl calls "collective trauma." Many cultures, suffering from such a collective trauma, degenerate into scapegoating.

Blaming is a glaring example of not being able to take responsibility. This book, however, focuses on certain genuine situations for which we are not responsible. Where does blame come in?

Through the agency of Compassionate Inquiry, the person who is addicted (or habituated) to blaming can quickly find him/herself back in childhood where whatever happened usually ended up being his/her fault. What's left of those childhood experiences is pain. The child knows "I didn't do it!" but was blamed anyway. As a grown-up, it doesn't matter what the issue is. A grown-up who was constantly blamed as a child will not accept responsibility in adulthood because responsibility is associated with being wrong. So the person continues their never-ending dance of blaming others.

What is required to stop this addicted cycle is love and compassion for that child who was actually not at fault. That childhood experience is where the solution to the problem lives. In order to get to it, there is one hurdle to pass through, however. The adult must find it in his/her own heart to embrace his/her own childhood self with love and compassion. But if the adult cannot find that love and compassion in themselves, the cycle of blame will continue.

Some adults, however, have access to their inner guidance. With inner guidance, I am able to accept responsibility. It is much easier for me to take responsibility for family and household matters than it is for a politician to take responsibility for a wrong decision or for a promise not kept. However, the very act of taking responsibility is a matter of my inner authenticity and, therefore, a matter of my emotional/mental health. Blaming others is a manipulation of the world outside me. Taking responsibility seems to be an acceptance of my inner power. It means I am not afraid to face my problems and will most likely overcome them. As long as I blame my problems on others, those problems will not be solved!

Self-Correction

Part 4: Everything That Happens Has a Reason

Being uncomfortable is not a problem. It is a teaching tool.
If I am following my inner guidance, I am likely to experience a lot of discomfort. This process is akin to body-building. I will know the cause of the discomfort! I will know that my previous reluctance to learn to live at peace with the unknown, with uncertainty, will result in a few extra "muscle aches"!

Accepting responsibility, for example, will likely bring me a lot of extra work. At least, it will for a while, until I learn to say "No!" The way I look at it, inner guidance is just another form of schooling. It is emotional schooling.   Since I already spent twenty-one years of my life in formal education, and since I already practice any number of disciplines to keep my body and mind fit, what is another twenty years to learn who I am?

If I prefer not to experience discomfort, I condemn myself to repeating the same mistakes, blunders, and self-harming behaviors that alerted me to seek inner guidance in the first place. While I am unconscious that

I have blocked my own inner guidance, I may not know, may not even believe, that everything that happens has a reason. But it does! And the reason is relational! I have a constant relationship with myself, and I have an ongoing relationship with any number of people. My relationships set up a pattern and become predictable.

When I was a child, at the most fundamental level, my interactions with my parents were not 'relational' as far as I was concerned. It seemed to be a one-way street. They were scared and anxious. I picked that up from them and made it my own, because that is how children operate. My parents did not tell me, "we are scared and anxious, but it will pass." They kept it to themselves, and they hid their emotions. They were most likely ashamed of their fears. They had no idea that a child could 'read' their emotions like an open book.

They also kept me scared and anxious by occasional punishments. This was usually a slap to the face or an actual spanking on my bottom, and most of it was unexpected. My relational interactions with my parents were based on fear and anxiety. I am sure they loved me, but I felt unloved, and so I adapted. I began to form personality traits that would hopefully please them. It was done totally unconsciously.

The reasons for the way in which I, as an adult, conduct all my interactions with myself and with other people, are basically two-fold. One, to please others so they would like me, and two, to punish myself, because I still feel unlovable, and being punished is part of my childhood comfort zone. Even as an adult, my relational beliefs and emotions are unconscious. When I was discharged from the US Army and settled into a central Philadelphia rooming house and felt nothing, it was because I was living an emotionally unconscious life.

Self-Correction

Part 5: Resolving Conflict.

What kind of 'neighborhood' do I create in my own mind? What is my personal evolution/development?

I am talking about what goes on inside my own mind. It is not at all unusual for me to take on contradictory philosophies, or say one thing but do something else.

So if I take my children out to a march for world peace, and then when we reach home and we are all tired, I yell at them for getting in my way, I am sending them (and myself) a contradictory message. My wish to have my children grow up supporting world peace takes a nosedive. I yell at my children again to make less noise because "mommy's asleep" and then sit down and let the television blare because I cannot sleep. Unconscious of my relational environment (my 'neighborhood'), I have become insensitive. I teach my children basic hypocrisy.

The conflict is within me. How do I deal with it? I have read books on conflict resolution and more or less know how it works among 'civilized' people. Marshall Rosenberg has come up with a carefully constructed set of guidelines for non-violent communications:

1. Take time to observe the situation.
2. Express my feelings (not my perspective!).
3. Identify my needs (other than that I need to be soothed).
4. Request an action that is beneficial for all involved.

Now I wonder what happens to a person who participates in a conflict resolution program, and then does nothing to resolve their own internal conflict? Because that is exactly where I am!

Working towards inner guidance is one certain way to learn internal conflict resolution! Can I personalize those basic four steps?

1. Take time to observe myself. What is the conflict within me, and what body sensations are present?
2. Find my feeling within those body sensations (not my perspectives or judgments).
3. Identify my needs (and not my addictions).
4. Act on the most beneficial outcome.

Upholding Our Importance

In the *Art of Dreaming* Don Juan tells Carlos Castaneda, "… most of our energy goes into upholding our importance … if we were capable of losing some of that importance, two extraordinary things would happen to us. One, we would free our energy from trying to maintain the illusory idea of our grandeur; and two we would provide ourselves with enough energy to … catch a glimpse of the actual grandeur of the universe."

There is a major difference between 'upholding importance', and meaning. We can immediately recognize the former as an 'identity'. When I worked as a free-lance broadcaster for CBC Radio back in the early eighties, I arranged an interview with a Yale University Professor. When I arrived at his office, the very first thing he told me was that he was included in a particular *Who's Who* compilation. I was still living a rather unconscious, habituated life, but I could see right through his insecurity, and thought to myself that he probably paid to have himself included. His 'importance' was a survival issue. Victor Frankl called it 'meaning' rather than self-aggrandizement. In a concentration camp self-aggrandizement is useless. But meaning becomes important.

My reaction (even though it was silent), was triggered by this Professor overstating his 'importance'. You see, I had already carried great respect for him, or at least for his knowledge, because he had earned his Ph.D., landed a tenured professorial position, had co-authored a book that was on my own curriculum, and had articles published in various journals. But after hearing about his being in a *Who's Who*, I lost all respect for him. Moreover, he was boring and I could not include his interview in the final cut of my program.

As for meaning, Victor Frankl provided a wonderful definition in his book, *A Search for Meaning*. He was in a German concentration camp during World War II, and was a trained Psychiatrist. What he noticed was that everyone among the Jewish prisoners around him found a different perspective as to why they were there, and how they might survive. They were looking for a meaning, and in spite of all the odds, each found one that suited his/her need.

Why am I Afraid to Ask for a Date?

Part 1: I am Too Shy

OK, not everyone is out there is seeking a date, or making a play to connect with someone. So those of you who are happily married, please skip this chapter!

When I was in high school, "Whistler" was the ultimate 'ladies' man' and was not at all bothered with rumors about whom he was dating or what they were doing together. He was the star of our high school football team. I was a member of the Audio-Visual Club.

I really don't need to say anything about why I was not surrounded by young, budding girls. I simply did not dare to ask anyone for a date. If I just spoke to a girl I liked, I became flustered, turned red in the face, and embarrassed myself.

I thought I was too shy. I masturbated often. But I longed for that female touch.

Fifteen years later I had dinner with two former classmates who had married in the meantime.

"Do you want to know what the girls thought of you in High School?" the wife asked.

"Of course," I said, curious.

"We heard stories of you dating a gorgeous Hungarian girl from a Philadelphia design college, and thought you wouldn't ask anyone local for a date because we weren't good enough for you."

That was a surprise for me. The only part of that 'rumor' that was true, was that my mother had invited a Hungarian family for a Summer picnic. That family, indeed, had a daughter who was around my age, and she was drop-dead gorgeous. She did, in fact, attend a Philadelphia design school.

Our family friendship grew. They invited us to their city home, and we invited them to our "Pennsylvania Dutch" small town many times over several years.

In retrospect, it was not difficult to see how the word went out that I was dating this girl. I also cannot deny that I was head-over-heels in love with her. Unfortunately, my fears, and my shyness, prevented me from even having a good conversation with her. Instead I carried on great conversations with her parents!

And here I thought I wasn't good enough for the local girls!

The negative outcome of even thinking about asking someone for a date can have many perspectives with unintended possibilities! The main problem, of course, is fear of rejection.

Why am I Afraid to Ask for a Date?

Part 2: Fear of Rejection

If I am too shy, that is my interpretation of my own projection. What am I hiding from myself? I don't want to confront my fear. Why?

Because confronting my own fear hurts. Someone pointed out a line in the *Tibetan Book of the Dead*, which said, more or less, "Face your pain. If you don't face it, it will become worse!" (Chapter 33, last paragraph; also Chapter 76). It was only three or four years ago when this 'ultimatum' appeared to me.

If fear causes me pain, in the Buddhist sense, it is a demon. I had already mentioned the story of the Buddha, sitting alone, surrounded by the fiercest demons you could imagine. What must have occurred to him was that very fact: if I have to imagine demons, they don't actually exist. I can believe in demons, but if I do, they exist and will plague me.

There is also a Christian association with demons. Jesus went around casting out demons. He was not afraid.

Does that mean I have to treat my fear of asking for a date as if it was a demon? It is just one possibility.

What is the real problem? Was I afraid of being rejected prior to wanting to ask a high school girl for a date?

Yes! If fear is a demon, then I have been carrying one around for most of my life!

I grew up in the1950s Budapest, where young boys played soccer everywhere. My father and I even played in our tiny living room. It is little wonder that at the Summer Olympics of 1952, Hungary won the Gold Medal. Puskas, the team Captain, was more important than Stalin. At least he was to us, the young soccer boys.

But for the young ones, playground and street soccer were our daily fare. When it came to choosing who was going to play on which team, the known, strong players were chosen first. Between the ages of 7 to 12, I was a thin, scrawny, and often ill boy. I wanted to play soccer so badly, but I only got onto a team, even a four-person side street 'team', because of friends. If I did not have a friend present, I was not chosen. I was rejected.

The same thing happened on American sand-lots. Joseph Chilton Pearce wrote at length about an aspect of our brain development that kicks in around the age of seven. We learn the concept of 'fairness'. He noted that children will argue endlessly before playing. Their topic? What team-distribution was fair! These arguments sometimes took much longer time than the game itself! Being left out of that process by not being picked to play at all was like becoming an outcast.

So my fear of rejection goes right back to not being a very powerful football player, in spite of the fact that I believed I was a world-class player already! By the next day, I had to suppress that fear (unconsciously, of course) in order to insinuate myself into the next lineup.

Why am I Afraid to Ask for a Date?

Part 3: Rejection and the Fear of Abandonment

Being rejected at any given time, really has nothing to do with what is happening at that moment.

The process is similar to a physical illness. By the time the illness manifests, months and years of stress had taken its inevitable toll. The medical doctor then treats the manifested symptom and the stress goes untreated.

What I actually perceive, unconsciously, when I face the potential of rejection, is a projection of what happened to me when my mother went to the bathroom, even for a minute, and I, as an infant, no longer saw her. In that infant mindset, my mother literally disappeared. My survival responses 'believed' that she would never come back, I would never be fed again, and that I would die.

Two fears, therefore, have influenced most of my relationships throughout my life. The first was abandonment. The second was a 'learned' fear because all the people around me were afraid for their lives, and I had no choice but to pick up, or learn their fear because that is what they 'gave' me instead of love and compassion. All young children internalize their parents' emotions, or the emotions of whoever is in their presence.

Because I had not yet considered that the pain becomes worse each time I get myself in the same situation, I remained unconscious of that fear until recently, and it has caused me internal problems. These problems include minor chronic inflammations in my muscles, the occasional but repeated sinus infections, and gum disease. Each can be dealt with medically, but the ongoing inflammation, I believe, is a direct result of my unresolved fears.

The process of resolving emotional trauma, however, has begun. It is not a healing. It is a learning process, which teaches me that I don't have to harm myself every time someone says "No!" to me. Life goes on quite well, actually! My current reality does not change the fact that I was mortally afraid of rejection by girls as a teenager. That was a fact of my life. My current reality means that I no longer am afraid of being rejected in my relational interactions. Or, if that fear occasionally returns, I stop, take a breath, and deal with it. I reassure the scared child within me that I love myself and hold myself with self-compassion.

Why am I Afraid to Ask for Information?

While I was studying for a Master's Degree, I learned to drive a dump truck and assured myself of a good paying summer job. In spite of my newly-mastered truck-handling, one day I dumped a load of gravel on a street corner I believed I was instructed to, but it turned out to be the wrong location.

When I showed up for the next run, the boss looked around and asked me where the gravel was. I gave him the location and watched as he first looked at me dumbfounded, then slowly let loose a stream of expletives and belittling statements that questioned my sanity, my father's sanity, and my inability to follow directions.

By the time I returned to graduate school as a 'mature student', I was relatively self-confident and comfortable within myself—at least in the working world. Without meaning any harm, I simply responded to my boss with the words, "You told me to dump the gravel on that corner."

I was immediately fired.

I didn't have a single opening in my demeanor for the possibility of being wrong. I don't remember if I had any doubts about the dump location, but a bit of humility and double-checking for the right site might have helped me.

The net result was that I ended up hauling asphalt for a road construction crew and earned twice as much for the rest of the summer than I would have with the smaller, private contractor. This story is not here to promote the forgetting of instructions. I am sure, however, that I can make use of it somewhere as an act of 'divine guidance'. "Accept your mistake! What follows is a gift from your Inner Guide!" Or something like that.

My takeaway? This occasion of not double-checking for information worked out for my long-term benefit. However, the key here for me, was my attitude that I couldn't be wrong. Now I can see this attitude as something I absorbed and adopted from my father, the "man who knew everything!"

That inflexibility has caused me more trouble over my lifetime than most other interpersonal, relational attitudes.

Why Am I Afraid to Ask When I Want to?

In my late twenties I was living in Toronto, Ontario, Canada, struggling to master the ancient Egyptian hieroglyphic, hieratic and demotic scripts. To give myself a break, I attended a philosophical discussion group every Sunday morning at the Toronto Lodge of the Rosicrucian Order, AMORC.

I had lots of training, undergraduate courses in Philosophy, varied religious experience and a personal interest in spirituality. One of the goals of The Rosicrucian Order was to help its members transform the 'mystical' into a trusted, every-day experience.

I was hooked and had question after question to ask, and sometimes comments to make. But I remained silent for months.

The reason I remained silent is because every time I stood up to say something, I turned beet red, my heart seemed to pump in my throat, and did not let either air or words come through. When I would finally regain my ability to speak, I had forgotten what I was going to say. It was all too embarrassing. I forced myself to stand up and speak, and over the course of a year, I learned to breathe so that I would not enter an emotional paralysis.

I also took a ten-week Toastmasters course, which gave me the confidence to embark on a lifetime of public speaking and broadcasting.

Now, decades later, having dealt with some of my repressed, unconscious trauma, I can see myself as having lived under the terror of my father's abuse. As a child, his derogatory remarks every time I opened my mouth and said something used to cut me to the core. I ended each attempt believing that I was inadequate, unworthy, and useless. It was actually even worse than that! Each interaction with my father made me feel terrorized. Ultimately, I felt that I was unloved.

Of course, I did not connect with that childhood fear and belief during these philosophical discussions. These memories were deeply repressed. I was just ashamed of myself. I came out of the Toastmasters' course feeling loquacious and self-confident. I went on to a career of lecturing, and radio and television interviews, all without a hint of the great difficulty I used to have. I did not solve my childhood emotional problems, but I learned new coping mechanisms, and new adaptations.

Asking for clarification, though, is still difficult. The specter of my father's terror is still somewhere within me. I no longer feel the terror, just a tinge of hesitancy and the rising of shame. Even regarding a subject that I cannot possibly know the details of, if someone asks me about it, there is a thought in me that I should know. That thought is actually my father's attitude that he knew everything.

What is the Downside of Believing You Know Everything?

The Story

When I was a child, I had the impression that my father knew everything. He seemed to believe that he did. Later on in life I heard that it was a common Hungarian and German delusion that an 'educated' person would know everything there was to know. However, that custom was no longer tenable. Goethe may have been the last person on earth who may have known everything, since the number of books that existed in his day could have been read in a lifetime. By the time Goethe died, publishing had exploded, and it was no longer possible for one person to read everything, much less to know everything.

My father, along with millions of other German and Hungarian men, remained unaware of this unbridgeable gap. When I 'divorced' him in 1956, he seemed to develop a tinge of respect for me. He wrote me a wistful letter asking about all the things I was learning in the United States. He even undertook English lessons and learned to speak and write English, possibly in anticipation of our meeting again.

That meeting actually took place exactly ten years later. I had just graduated from university and spent part of the summer in Paris. An English friend called me and offered me a ride to Budapest. I accepted on the spur of the moment. Two days later, I went into the building where I had spent my childhood, walked up to the third floor and rang the familiar doorbell.

I was very nervous, needless to say, and did not have any particular script in mind. It was just as well, because of what happened next! The door opened. It was my father. He looked at me and without hesitating, asked,

"Can I help you?"

I was speechless. That response was the last thing I would have expected. I was not prepared for it! I managed to squeak out,

"Father, it is me, Daniel, your son!"

At that point the surreal moment just continued. His face contorted into some kind of 'Oh My God' grimace, except that he was an atheist. Then he caught himself and became humble. He opened the door wide, asked me to come in and introduced me to his new family. He began to ask me one question after another, mostly about what I wanted. How could he make me more comfortable? What could he do for me?

This humbleness continued for the few years that he lived. When I paid my father the next visit, he fell all over himself taking me wherever I wanted to go, and buying me the best meals. I love Hungarian food, so I appreciated it. He even insisted on buying me a suit, which I did not need, but accepted after many "No, thank you," scenes. The reality was that I could not wear that suit back home, no matter how unconscious I pretended to be about fashion.

Whereas at the time I did not understand the nature of his humility towards me, I clearly saw the contrast between his new behavior and his former all-knowing attitude. I also accepted the fact that I didn't want to grow up to be a "know-it-all!"

The temptation was certainly there. I had far more education than my father ever had. I had traveled widely, whereas his world was limited to Germany, Austria and Hungary, mostly during the Second World War. The need within me to remain 'unlike' my father was so strong that

I squashed all tendencies toward arrogance the moment I became aware of them. Instead of showing off my knowledge, I embarked on a path of "wisdom" and became a storyteller, first and foremost to my own children.

Yet, the spectre of arrogance haunted me most of my life. It was projected by my self-confidence. Most people could not separate my self-confidence from arrogance. In a way, I fuelled the projection by joking to my friends that, "I can take the wrong road totally confidently until it becomes obvious that I am lost." My confidence remained, not in whether or not I was on the right road, but rather, in the fact that I knew how to turn around; how to correct my mistake.

Years later, I talked about my father to a friend. She listened to the story of my relationship with my father, thought about it for a while, then turned to me and said, "You know, when you surprised your father with your first unexpected visit, and he didn't recognize you, something deeply disturbing happened to him. The man who knew everything, did not know his own son. That must have been traumatic for him. That could have been what humbled him."

CHAPTER

115

Courage

Part 1: Definition

In Chapters 89-91 I have examined parent-child relationships. I know these chapters have just skimmed the surface as volumes have been written on that one topic! But in Chapter 91, just one act of courage in a mother-son relationship literally healed the heart.

That is exactly what "courage" means, from the French word, "coeur", which means "heart". 'Courage', therefore, means 'heartfulness'. In this case, it means acting with heartfulness with our children. Anything less borders on deceit.

Courage

Part 2: Can I Handle Pain?

Most therapists exist because I can't handle pain. In fact, all addictions develop as a result of us not being able to handle our pain! Why do I have pain in the first place?

I am talking about emotional pain, of course. Every time a situation arises where I am "not good enough," or "not worth it," or "not heard," or "not acknowledged, or end up feeling 'less than' someone else," I will most likely feel pain. I will also most likely not acknowledge that pain, immediately cover it up and come out fighting and raging instead. In my habituated, unconscious reaction to soothe my pain, I lose contact both with my abuser-the person who triggered me-and also with my own emotional center.

What we have now learned after millennia of passing on generational abuse to our children is that separation from my authentic self is the real cause of emotional pain.

Belittling 'games' go on between parents and children, between siblings, in school, at the workplace, and especially in nursing homes where many of the elderly who need care are helpless and at the mercy of their care-givers. Each abuse causes, or brings up, deep emotional pain.

As children, we cannot live with pain. All children repress their pain unconsciously, otherwise they would not survive!

But psychological abuse tends to continue throughout our lives until I, at any given point in my life, take a deep breath and declare my independence!

Again, this declaration is an act of courage. By slowing down and taking a moment to assess what the other person said to me, I open a door to clarity! The other person's words are more about them than they are about me. The need to repress pain is a childhood need, not an adult need.

The jump from childhood needs to adult needs does not always happen!

Why is that? Because hardly anyone has made that jump! Because the 'abuser' is actually speaking from his or her own pain without even knowing it. Instead of slowing down to consider why, as a parent, a sibling, schoolmate, a co-worker, a boss or a caregiver, they would say something belittling to me, they habitually and totally unconsciously spew out their venom at me.

The jump from childhood needs to adult needs does not usually happen because hardly anyone role models it!

The way we treat each other drives us crazy! There is only one rule.

"I cannot change someone else's behavior. I can only change mine."

So it is up to me to slow down and take a moment to appreciate the larger picture. Increasing my own self-awareness is the only remedy that allows me to see that my 'abusers' are talking about themselves, not me; that my 'abusers' are talking from their own pain; that my 'abusers' have no idea what they are doing; that my 'abusers' are acting unconsciously!

I don't need to feel hurt. I am buoyed by my own enthusiasm for life. I am held by my own, now developed, authentic emotional self. I can live and cope with any emotional pain and trauma that come along.

Many people who are abused with such acts of belittling, fight back. The anger of "being made to feel hurt" is real. The resolution, however, rests in those very words with which I accuse my abuser. When I say, or even think or believe, that someone can "make me feel hurt," I empower my abuser.

No! Nobody has the ability to make me feel emotionally hurt! I have to willingly allow that to happen. Unfortunately, during my childhood I came to accept that others can "make me feel hurt." As I became an adult, I continued that belief without ever questioning it. I have even amassed evidence to prove that all sorts of people can make me feel hurt. I totally accept that process as 'true'. But just because I accept a belief, it doesn't mean it is a universal truth. It is an unexamined process. It is an unconscious, recurring life experience that can be changed. It can be changed by knowledge, and by an act of courage.

Courage

Part 3: Can I Hurt Other People?

This question is the corollary of the previous chapter about whether or not (and how often) I am hurt by others. And, just as it is true that I get hurt, it is also true that I hurt others. That is the source of most of my guilt.

However, just as I don't need to be hurt and I don't need to be "made to feel hurt," others don't need to feel hurt when I speak to them.

A dance teacher and her husband had been living together for seven years during a long and initially happy marriage, without having anything to do with each other except for paying the bills.

I asked her, "If you are on talking terms, tell him you want to separate and eventually divorce and get on with your life!"

The horrified look on her face was precious.

She said, "What will our children say? I don't want to make my parents and his parents feel bad." As her objections continued, it became clear that they were all about her fear of hurting other people.

"What about you?" I asked. "Where is your sense of self-compassion and self-care, to do something that will pull you out of this seven-year slump? How long do you need to suffer because you assume other people will be hurt if you break out to find a sense of happiness?"

She hung her head and it was obvious that, for the moment, I had said enough. But the seed was planted, and within a year she found the courage to amicably tell her husband that she was leaving.

"What is the problem?" he asked. "We have a perfectly functioning marriage, a perfectly functioning household, what's wrong?"

Within a month, when we met at a business-coaching check-in session, she was all smiles. "My parents were in total favor of my separation. My in-laws not only understood, but invited me to come over any time. And my children? They said, 'It's about time!'"

At our business-coaching sessions we had both learned to be assertive—to say what we mean without hesitation—but without the aggression that would threaten others. In other words, we learned to say what we mean authentically and with courage. People respond well to the heart's truth. Even if they don't like the answer, they are not intimidated when it is from the heart. They have a choice to respond with their own heartfelt truth and begin to negotiate, or they can accept what we say at face value.

The bottom line is that I cannot be hurt, nor can I hurt others. Not unless I deliberately set out to do so! The fact that I had bought into a belief system that says others can hurt me, may have been true in childhood. Just as I had given up my authenticity in childhood for the sake of attachment in order to survive in childhood, I can now take back my authenticity and no one gets hurt any more. I am an adult now. I don't have to function on childhood survival instincts.

Courage

Part 4: How Deep Does it Go?

What is the relationship between courage and responsibility? Is it like a proportional relationship, where the more courageous I become the more responsible I become? Or, is it possible that there is no relationship at all?

I had recently practiced Compassionate Inquiry with a client who brought with him an interesting conundrum. He is incapacitated but has a modest independent income. At the same time, he depends on his wife to complete the financial support to run the household.

The issue he brought was that he tends to blame his wife when his own sense of taking on responsibility overwhelms him. I stopped his story right there. I didn't need to hear any more, because he had already given me two concepts that I could ask questions about for hours! In turn, he could continue his stories for hours. We both needed to focus.

The two concepts were 'blame' and 'responsibility'.

"What do you see as the relationship between 'blame' and 'responsibility'?" I asked my client.

Deadly silence. That was good. He was thinking.

"Oh … My … God …," he said slowly. "A responsible person would not resort to blame."

"Bingo!" I probably shouldn't have said that, but what the hell, it was out. "So you just told me two perceptions of yourself. One, that you blame your wife, and the other that your are 'overwhelmed by responsibility.'"

My client nodded. So I continued. "Neither of these is wrong. That is just how you operate your life at the moment. It is what it is. Can you see how they are related?"

"That is what blows me away," my client said. "When I was three years old, my father had a stroke. He survived, but from that moment on we had to take care of him. My mother and aunts earned the money, my baby sister was still at my mother's teats, but I had an older sister, 9, who already had a career in child theatre. We were told that we each had to contribute to the financial strength of the family. My job was to take care of my father. And I did, without questioning it. But whenever a bill came in that we did not have enough money to pay, my mother began to complain, and to blame everyone, including me, that we were not contributing enough! I began to feel guilty about not contributing enough. I took on more and more responsibility until I became overwhelmed. As I grew up, I started to blame everyone else for the financial mess around me. I am still doing it. I am still the three-year-old, helpless boy looking after his debilitated father!" A moment later he exploded. "Shit! I have become handicapped just as he was. Was it my three-year-old 'self' who obediently role-modeled his father?"

We both got it that his question was rhetorical. I asked, "If you could, what would you say to the helpless, bewildered three-year-old boy to relieve his burden?"

"Boy, you have it tough! You have it real tough." My client paused, and took a deep breath. "You are supposed to have a care-free childhood, and you are caught up acting the role of your father to your father. What a farce! What did you know about how to be a father at three? Everybody was busy keeping the finances together, and you believed you had a responsibility for that too when you were blamed for shortfalls. You learned that endless cycle of blame and guilt and accepted it. Who loved you?"

"Yes," I repeated his question, "Who loved you?"

"Nobody," he said, and tears came to his eyes. Tears came to my eyes, too.

"Who will love that child now?" I asked.

"There is no one but me," my client said.

"How can you love him," I asked, "this three year old child still trying to fulfill his responsibilities, but still becoming overwhelmed and resorting to a cycle of guilt and blame?"

"If I was really responsible," my client said, "I would not be blaming anyone!"

The session continued with the client devising meetings between his 'adult' self and 'child' self with the singular goal of reassuring the child 'self' that he is now both safe and loved, surrounded by adult compassion, and is free to give up his fifty year struggle to make sense of a senseless cycle.

Somewhere, deep within himself, my client found the courage to invite his own stuck child, who was still repeating a cycle that began as a survival role, to participate in an aware, awakened world of love and compassion.

I don't know if he can pull it off! I don't know whether or not the next financial crisis at home will catapult him back into the cycle, within which he knew what to do! But I know he has found the tools for a different, gentler coping mechanism.

Meaning

A spiritual website on the internet states unequivocally, "There is meaning beyond measure in everything in life."*

"Where?" you might ask. It is our perceptions and our way of interpreting life that produce both 'reality' and meaning. Reality and meaning, 'out there', are ultimately glimpses of the reality and meaning deep within us.

In turn, our perceptions and interpretations are based either on our unconscious belief system, or on our conscious, aware, non-judgmental, neutral mind.

How do I get from one to the other? How do I stop believing that my projection, which forms the world out there, is an illusory reality? How do I begin to stop the judgments, and the prejudices and develop a neutral mind?

I have created a myth as to who I am. But it is not a stagnant, fossilized myth. I add my experiences to it all the time, and so the myth continues to evolve.

Let's take for example, the myth of the American West. As the historian Richard White once wrote, "The mythic West imagined by Americans has shaped the West of history just as the West of history has helped create the West Americans have imagined." (https://www.nytimes.com/2019/03/09/style/cowboy-poets-elko-nevada.html#keepreadingelko)

Where does this phenomenon come from? Dr. Gabor Maté provides us with a surprising answer: "The Buddha said in the Dhammapada that with our minds and thoughts we create the world. He was the first great psychologist, who understood the power of implicit memory, perception, and interpretation. People create a world with their perceptions, and then they respond not to what's happening, but to the world that they created in their minds.

'The part that Buddha didn't say is that before our minds create the world, the world creates our mind. The mind by which we create the world, was first created in response to our early experiences. The world programs us. From then on, we are doomed to live in that world, until we see that now we are the ones who are creating it." (Quoted with permission from Compassionate Inquiry Phase 2 Course, Module 1: "We create the world"© 2018 Gabor Maté MD and Sat Dharam Kaur ND. page 16)

If I am content with reacting to the world around me, and the people in it with my existing belief system, then I don't need to change. If my current set of beliefs serve me and produce happiness within me, why would I want to change? If my life is full of meaning with authentic friends around me, then there is no need to change anything. What are the chances?

My unconscious belief system is based on many, many terrible experiences that I have had while I was young. My beliefs are based: on having been abandoned time and again, not being heard (told to shut up over and over again), not being acknowledged, being made to feel valueless and insignificant, being physically and emotionally abused (and, for many people, sexually abused) and the list can go on and on. Such experiences produce a set of beliefs that will skewer my perceptions and make me look upon the world as dangerous, hostile and threatening.

Combined with my own survival tools, fight, flight, or freeze, and the natural functions of my medulla and the amygdala, which form our warning system for what can go wrong, my outlook on life is mostly defensive. I will expect things to go wrong, for people to attack me, to fail in my projects, and so on. These beliefs will result in a behavior where, no matter which survival tool I am using, fear, anger and conflict will plague me all my life!

My other choice is to examine my belief system. A system which was superimposed on me before I could even talk, and certainly before I could think and make choices. The truth is that I was and am responsible for none of those beliefs!

It is only when I make my own choices, based on observing the world around me, and evaluating what works and what doesn't, that meaning forms. I have to put an effort into observing my life in order for it to be meaningful.

*http://heavenletters.org/in-gods-image.html

Redemption

Part 1: Who Needs Redemption?

Would you read a novel or a romance, or even a murder mystery if the characters had no failings? I think such a book would be dull and boring. What makes us human beings 'interesting' is that we are full of faults and failings! We make mistakes. Some of us, however, want to make up for or correct some of our mistakes. This drive to clear the slate, to make amends, and therefore to feel worthy, is called "redemption."

As I read fiction or a biography, I look for the weaknesses of the character and see if anyone in the novel, or the focus of the biography, sought—and perhaps found—redemption. It is the seeking of redemption that makes a work of fiction (or any story) so gripping!

I recently asked myself the question, "Why am I so interested in fictional characters seeking redemption? Why am I reading novel after novel, mystery after mystery, and seem to need more?"

Then it dawned on me. I am the one who needs to seek redemption! I have simply externalized, or projected my need onto these novels, the reading of which are a 'safe' encounter with redemption—if and when it takes place.

CHAPTER

121

Redemption

Part 2: How Do I Begin to Seek Redemption?

I find it strange that, while I expect my fictional characters to seek and find redemption, there are few books on the market offering the way to redemption, except strictly Christian books that offer only one way, through Jesus Christ.

One of these few is *Getting Real: The Road to Personal Redemption* by Kevin Robinson and Dick Todd.

The authors write by way of introducing their work on Amazon.com, "Getting Real is all about rediscovering who we really are, and living our life based on that reality rather than on the one our minds often create for us. Though we hate to admit it, our day-to-day self-image can be a very skewed drama based on fears, projections, misperceptions, misinformation, and, well, bullshit. There's just no better word for it. If our lives are bogged down in B.S., then it's almost impossible to be real about ourselves and/or about the people and the world around us. So Getting Real is actually just a new approach to that mirror we are often so prone to avoid. It's not about our being wrong, or bad, or even deliberately dishonest with ourselves. Instead, Getting Real is, about training ourselves to recognize and reject the B.S. that often seeps into our lives."

Getting real is becoming authentic, and reconnecting with the Self I lost when my need for attachment trumped my need to be authentic as a young child who was totally dependent on my parents. Whether I was six months old and I lost sight of my mother, or I was three years old and my mother was angry at me, my survival instincts kicked in. Those instincts were the only tools I had as a child, and I tried to do anything and everything to win back the contact and/or the love of my parents. In the process of doing that, I abandoned my authenticity.

It may be difficult to imagine that I have lived a fairly long life without being connected to my authentic self. I still had a moral base. I knew the difference between right or wrong, and the truth or a lie, but I was mostly unconscious of what was going on inside myself. The emotional development, which should have been my birthright, had stopped as soon as I began to repress my emotions as a child, and I began to adapt manipulative ways to re-establish contact with my parents.

Redemption, in this sense, is the re-establishment of contact with my own authentic self. This inner struggle is much more prevalent in non-fiction books. The fact is that I cannot describe my struggles with my inner pain clearly, until I face my inner pain, sit with it, and find an adaptation to cope with that inner pain without destroying myself. Compassionate Inquiry is one avenue for that redemption.

Technically, any book on emotional readjustment, compassion and spiritual growth has something to do with redemption.

I sought out these books because I felt stuck with something I could not name. I sought out spiritual training and meditation because I was restless about the emotional imbalance I felt within myself. However, I don't know what brought about my restlessness. What focused my attention on what is going on within me were key authors or lecturers who came into my life at a time when I needed help, and was willing to listen. Redemption was the emotional/behavioral changes I went through based on what I learned.

In the novels I read, often the main character, who is usually in despair, hits rock bottom, pulls himself/herself together and begins the long climb out. In real life, hitting rock bottom often ends up in suicide. Depression can create the sort of hormonal imbalance wherein the meaning of life disappears. It is usually a momentary state. But many people don't wait, or cannot wait, for it to pass.

Redemption

Part 3: How Do I Find Redemption?

R e-read this book!

Who Am I?

Part 1: Who Am I as Far as You are Concerned?

This question has been woven into almost every chapter of this book! But I can fine-tune the answer. I have to be aware of who I am, in order to see how I respond to my environment, and in particular, how I interact with people. If I don't know who I am, I will interact with my environment and with people in a mostly unconscious way. Unconscious interaction with others is the formula for constant suffering!

Who am I?

Is it a matter of 'who I am as far as you are concerned?'

Or is it a matter of who I think I am?

You see, as a human being, I tend to project an image of how I want you to see me! That habit of projection means that I believe I have something to hide and manage. I believe that I am holding a secret, a feeling of dread, a shame, an embarrassment, a vulnerability, or whatever it is that I don't want you to know. My entire life was focused on creating my image or my facsimile, for you! In fact, I was so busy creating and managing that "image" that I had no idea who I really was.

Projecting an image to protect my vulnerability was (and is) a strong drive. My tendency was to ignore who I really was underneath the nice clothes, the clean, manicured look, the affectations of power and sophistication. Even if I was to claim that I don't indulge much in self-care, other than keeping myself hygienic, I still would like you to see me somewhat differently than I believe I really look.

I use these conditional words on purpose. I "would like you to see me" is a managed way of presenting myself, as if I am a master of illusion.

Not to worry, we are all magicians, and masters of illusion. The trouble is that we tend to believe our own illusions! However, it is this very effort to manage how you see me that separates me from my emotional center in this very moment! It is this same effort to manage how you see me that separates me from you!

In essence, who I am may not be any different from who I was at six months old, or perhaps three years old. I am still trying to manipulate you to love me, because I cannot love myself.

Who Am I?

Part 2: Pretending to Be "Objective"

While managing how I want you to see me, I also project a level of sophistication. I pretend I am beyond emotions. I pretend to see the world objectively.

This is the point where my illusions about myself begin to unravel. To see the world objectively is to deny my emotions.

My culture tends to reinforce my pretenses! Newspaper and other media reporters claim to tell the news objectively. Scientific research and judicial system spokespersons claim they are being objective in their research and judgments.

Yet, there is no human being who is devoid of emotions. We are sentient beings and most of us are scared to death of our own emotions. We hide and repress them.

At best, then, 'hidden' and 'repressed' emotions are being interpreted as 'objective'.

The "life coaching" business, for one, has come up with the concept of the "neutral mind." To reach this state of neutrality, however, I have to know myself, practice being in the moment, yet remain aware that I am a sentient, emotional being.

Who Am I?

Part 3: I Am a Body With Feelings

Who I am, of course, has nothing to do with the image I project. No matter how clever I become at building and dangling a doctored-up image of myself in front of you, I only do it because I don't know myself. On the physical level I am a bundle of bones and muscles, organs and blood vessels, nerves and an array of cells in an ever-increasing order of complexity and interdependence.

Each cell in this body is a veritable sensory organ attuned to more input than I can imagine. Each cell in my body is filled with bumps and cilia, and far more of them than one would expect. If I have fifty trillion of these cells in my body and each cell has dozens of sensors, I have immense sensitivity.

My interpretation of this overabundance of sensory acuity defines me, and results in both my harmony within and the harmony (or lack of it) that I achieve in my contact and connection with you.

Depending on the overall sensory stimulation to which my fifty trillion (or more) cells respond, various endocrine glands secrete hormones into my blood stream. Those hormones keep 'telling' me what that sensory stimulation is about. Those hormones cause feelings. If I claim, "I can't feel anything!" I am saying either that I don't have any hormones in my body, or that I have repressed my feelings and lost touch with my body.

Who am I if I have lost touch with feelings in my body?

Who Am I?

Part 4: I Am Potentially Omniscient!

The possibility that my sensory systems are able to detect the entire spectrum of frequencies the (ever expanding) universe produces, makes me omniscient!

I am not saying that I am omniscient in the way that my father thought he knew everything. I know it sounds like that, but I like to believe that I have put a sophisticated twist or a spiritual spin on it. Or that my current knowledge-base is well balanced with a sense of humor. In any case, I put you on notice, as a reader, that I chose to write this book in the first person hoping you would put yourself into the printed "I". That proposition still stands.

I am not saying that each one of us is conscious of all stimuli available in our universe! My consciousness, which is a sum total of the stimuli my fifty to a hundred trillion cells detect, makes my body and my 'consciousness' omniscient. The problem is that my brain functions can only interpret a small fraction of that vast array of frequencies. I can only handle a small percentage of what I am able to perceive and interpret. That fraction, then, becomes my 'reality'—my life.

The clear fact is that you and I have access to ALL the sensory stimuli, to all the information that has ever been felt, and to all the experiences and thoughts, said, written or imagined.

On the one hand, I have the potential to be omniscient, but my culture has elevated "omniscience" to the divine realms. To claim to be omniscient is to claim to be God. Many people do, at least on the basis that the Bible tells us we were created in the image of God. On the other hand, I am so handicapped that it's like I have all the strings of a piano keyboard available to me, but I keep playing only two octaves of it, and denying the other strings exist! If I limit myself due to my fear of what those other octaves might sound like, there is no danger of claiming omniscience.

Let's say that I believe and insist that my two octaves are all there is in the entire universe. I keep playing and managing those two octaves, and pretend to know them more than anyone else. I pretend to have exclusive access and special knowledge of each note even when the string breaks or goes out of tune. But I am not aware that at the same time I am playing, my emotions are playing on all the keys, not just the two octaves of which I am aware. Eventually I forget that everyone 'hears' all my notes, in tune or out, no matter what I say I am playing. I would become boring, or perhaps authoritarian and try to superimpose my two octaves on everyone else, claiming that if they 'hear' more than two octaves, they are crazy— or worse, mentally ill and must be locked up. That is what emotional repression does to people.

I don't need to pretend there is only a limited range of notes (emotions) available to me. In a universe of energy, no one has exclusive ownership of any 'bandwidth' of frequencies, although radio and microwave frequencies have been 'assigned' to paying technological corporations. That 'ownership' does not interfere with my access to omniscience, except if I spend most of my time and attention on the limited technological bandwidths and exclude the rest of the universe.

I am omniscient, therefore I am divine. The fact is that I am not necessarily aware of it! But something within me is. And that means something within you is also omniscient and divine.

Every human being is omniscient, and therefore we are all divine. As many spiritual teachers are fond of saying, "We are divine beings having a human experience."

Who am I?

Part 5: How Do I Contact My 'Divinity'?

D ivinity is somehow connected with omniscience. The reason I suspect that I might be omniscient or all knowing, in spite of myself, is because with so many sensory units, let's say twenty five times the number of cells in my body, or somewhere in the 1.5 quadrillion range, my unconscious mind retains every bit of information my sensors have been picking up since I was conceived. And who knows, each DNA strand might also be a storage mechanism for the memory of those ancestors from whom I inherited them.

Unfortunately, my conscious mind has no idea what is in my unconscious mind! So I don't know if I actually have omniscience or divinity in me, but like a good Gnostic, I believe I can access that knowledge. I believe that I am able to know. Or, in the words of the French Lacanian Psychiatrist, William Théaux, "I am able to gnow!"

How am I able to 'gnow'? How am I able to access that vast body of knowledge that I have experienced and picked up since my conception?

Remembering my dreams is one way. Trusting my intuition is another. I can become aware that what I 'see' in others is actually what, or who, I am. I can listen to what I complain about and become aware of what judgments and criticisms I invent about other people. It will be all about me!

There are dozens of other ways, none of which are part and parcel of my educational system, and none of which are necessarily a part of my daily practice.

Meditation usually attracts stream-of-consciousness, the intrusive mental chatter of my unexpressed thoughts. Some forms of meditation, however, focus on reaching beyond the chatter and listening to my intuition.

Bruce Lipton, the biologist-turned-spiritual guru, proposed in his book, *The Biology of Belief*, that each cell in our body has shared its localized consciousness and entrusted our collective personal consciousness to take care of our bodies and lives. With this proposal he most likely also suggests that that collective consciousness (of the totality of our individual cells) forms our 'soul'.

I actually prefer that interpretation! And if that personal collective consciousness also forms my unconscious mind, then I propose that I have a trustworthy inner guidance system, which has the benefit of my welfare as its sole goal. The reason I choose that condition comes from a Quantum Physics theory, that every Quantum Field has only one goal: to return to balance. And just as every human being as a personal collective consciousness, or a soul, is energetically connected with every other human being in our world, the most benefit for my own welfare comes from being in harmony and balance with every other human being. Another way of saying the same thing is: Love you neighbor as yourself. And someone said that two thousand years ago, and for some reason this concept of mutually shared love somehow crept into most religions, then was duly repressed.

Who Am I?

Part 6: I am a Dualistic Being

It is possible that my consciousness, or awareness, is a combination of my intellect and intuition. But if I discount my intuition, I am only functioning at half-potential.

Psychology was born because people noticed that our awareness is generally limited. Freud noted that my consciousness has various levels and played with the possibilities. The Superego, for example, is the consciousness of my parents' voice from my childhood. My parents may be dead, but the way they treated me in childhood is the way I treat myself in adulthood. Because of my Superego, I constantly tell myself what I can do and I cannot do as if I were my own father or mother.

Jung jumped ahead of Freud (in my opinion) and saw the need to access the unconscious. He found one door into the unconscious that Jungian scholars still continue to use, which is the analysis of dreams. Dreams were important to Jung because of their symbols. Human beings have been making, or recognizing and interpreting symbols throughout history. In our dreams, scrying, seeing rare phenomena, being surprised by animals—in fact, almost anything either unusual, or constant and recurring can be interpreted as a symbol. The one thing that is certain is that the unconscious mind communicates through symbols. No matter how intellectually developed I am, I cannot 'understand' my unconscious mind's promptings with my rational mind. Yes, I can make lists of symbols, and find interpretations with my intellect, but when that symbol appears in my dream, its meaning for me might be entirely different than for someone else! To make this difference more poignant, Jung offered five major Archetypes and countless minor ones as potential personality types.

The question, "Who am I?" must be answered in light of my ability to balance my intellectual agility with my 'skill' at symbolic interpretation, or by using my intuition. We have no standards with which to judge our levels of intuition. All we know is that some people are more intuitive than others, and that not all rational people will accept intuition as real in spite of the fact that in scientific and academic circles it is usually accepted that discoveries come as a result of hard work and a large dose of intuition.

So I have this dualistic nature, not just between the left and right brain, but between my conscious mind and my unconscious mind, and between my rational brain functions and intuitive body responses.

This dualism, however, is a technical matter. Just as any vehicle is made up of many parts and it nevertheless functions as a whole, I also function as one being. If it is not my consciousness, then it is my instincts that drive me. Unfortunately, I tend to be unconscious to the point where it is the childhood survival instincts that drive or guide me. With my inner systems, the difference between being guided or driven is my emotional balance. If I become aware of my unresolved childhood trauma and release my repressed childhood emotions, I am likely to feel secure. That notion of 'security' has nothing to do with financial security! Learning to deal with unresolved childhood trauma lifts me from the fear of what could happen to the security that I will be able to cope with, even benefit from whatever happens. As Krishnamurti said, when he was asked what the most important thing in his life was, "To let it be."

When my emotions are mostly repressed, and are unconsciously let out, they tend to be harmful or even violent. I am likely to live a defensive, manipulative life, driven by fear of loss and hope of gain.

From the outside, though, there is every possibility that with so many sensors in my body, I am actually connected with everything in the universe. That is what the Quantum Theory suggests, that all Quantum Fields are connected. The fact is, though, that I cannot use individual connections. My consciousness cannot single out too much even among those fields that are within the reach of my five main senses.

When someone is full of rage and I pass by, I am able to sense that rage. Two people in love are hard to miss.

To look at this energy field that we are from a greater distance, we know that eruptions from the sun's corona interfere with the earth's energy field and produce 'northern lights'. These energies may interfere with electromagnetic instrumentation in our technology on one level. On another level, I can see them. All phenomena influence me at some level.

What About Astrology?

As long as I depend on Astrology on a daily basis to survive, I am on the verge of addiction. This is especially so if I look to Astrology for its predictive tendencies. If I want to know the future and I am using Astrology to control the outcome, I am showing my insecurities. Our entire culture with its institutions, corporations and governments, is centered on controlling, predicting, and ordering my life.

Astrology can become a tool for predicting averages and elections. I would love to see statistics to compare the predictive qualities of Astrology with polling.

Astrology, however, is not a tool for predicting the future.

Rather than being predictive, Astrology is a tool to use to consider influences. There are seven major 'players' or 'planets' in ten houses with predictable conjunctions and squares and so on. Already, the possibilities are 'astronomical' and we haven't yet considered the thousands of other stars, comets, and 'heavenly' phenomena, all of which exert some effect on me, however miniscule it may be.

The only reason to look to astrology for prediction or effects, is because the effects the seven planets have on our universe have been observed for thousands of years, written down and preserved. The Renaissance 'scientists' such as Giordano Bruno, Isaac Newton and others were all practicing Astrologers. Astrology is not a science. It is more a practice (like medicine) or a language. However, if someone has a precise time of birth (to the second) then particularly important events can be identified.

Where does that leave me?

Astrology is a reflective tool. Do the course and interactions of the planets and stars reflect our tendencies? They do. But it is a reflection, not my inner reality. In fact, as long as Astrology keeps me from exploring my inner reality, it keeps me from developing.

Astrology, then, is a possible tool for exploring my inner reality. How do I feel today when Mercury is retrograde and Uranus has entered Taurus? I don't know myself well enough to say. But I am observing myself ... and who knows what I will learn?

Astrology, then, can become a coping mechanism to deal with my pain. All of the coping mechanisms I have ploughed through in this book are just that, and they are not 'healing' mechanisms. Even though there is no law to say that someone might find 'healing' in their behavioral adaptations, we are basically still here, on earth, to learn how to cope with our pain.

What is a 'Reflection'?

What I see outside of myself reflects what I 'am' within me.

What I see, what I 'understand' of the world, forms a perspective, or an interpretation based on what I know, what I believe, and what my experiences had been.

When I refuse to see, or when I am unable to see my own, inner, emotional actualities, I project them onto others in the world outside of me. I see my own reflection in others—most likely unconsciously. But, because I refuse to see myself within, as I am, I cannot tell that the world I have projected onto others is actually the world within me. (See Chapter 52 and Karl Pribram's theories)

When I stop to think, to consider things, to mediate or reflect, I have a chance to catch this dilemma and begin to set it right. I begin to see that some of the 'wrongs' I am accusing others of doing, are actually my problems.

Trickster gods, like Mercury, can help me with becoming reflective. The 'now-you-see-me, now-you-don't nature of Mercury, and its apparent forward-backward motion have been fodder for many civilizations for thousands of years. Mercury has been embraced as a metaphor for the elusive true self that all human beings have.

The outside world mirrors my belief system only because the outside world is a projection of that part of my own true, authentic self, which I refuse to get to know! A reflection is an illusion.

As the Buddha said, "all is illusion."

Are We Light Beings?

Light and darkness work in a symbiotic relationship. We might tend to think that they are always in perfect harmony based on our notion of darkness and daylight. But scientifically, light is energy and darkness is a lack of it. One of the later surprises from astrophysicists was that the universe, even though it looks dark to us, is actually full of energy, mostly light beams. Our personal experience, though, is that wherever there is light, it may cast a shadow, but light will always clear darkness. Wherever light cannot reach remains in darkness. Metaphorically, if I am the light, wherever I go, I dispel darkness. At no time am I threatened by darkness. At no time do I have to fear darkness. If I fear darkness, it is because I have populated that darkness with terrors and made up reasons to fear it. Mostly, though, the 'terrors' of darkness are the unknown things and qualities I project into it.

If light is energy, is darkness an absence of energy? I would think so, except that astrophysicists have come up with 'dark matter' and 'black holes' that are basically a form of energy. When I turn off the light, there is still energy in the room.

In our world, we live in a cycle of light and darkness. For whatever reason, some human beings have chosen to fear the dark cycle. I am sure we could find statistical facts and figures that, let's say, violent crimes happen more often in darkness than in daylight. Darkness as 'dangerous' or 'evil' is a perspective that may be valid to many people, but meaningless to others. Darkness holds endless fascination for us and creative people keep coming up with new terrors it can hold. An entire entertainment industry has developed around its endless possibilities, both in physical reality and in its symbolic form. The iconic exchange between Darth Vader and his son, Luke Skywalker from the Star Wars series best illustrates the symbolic separation between light and darkness when the father invites the son to join him on the dark side. Perhaps I should capitalize the Dark Side.

Since children pick up their parents' feelings without words, if they see us afraid of the dark, they will grow up being afraid of the dark.

As a child, I have 'picked up' myths and wrong interpretations, and many useless belief systems. Carolyn Myss called these "tribal instructions." She strongly recommended that I examine and replace them with my adult sense of balance between intuition and reason. Soul-guidance, and the knowledge that I am a 'light-being' also help in this process.

Is the latter a belief system? No! It is no longer far-fetched to call myself a light-being! Scientists have been able to look at human cells under immense magnification and found that all our cells contain a 'tubule' that is connected with the 'tubules' of all other cells, and photons, or light beams, course through these 'tubules' as long as we live. We are truly light beings.

Do I Need a Physical Practice?

Do I Need to Have a Discipline?

In order to maintain a minimal level of health, everyone needs to exercise. It doesn't matter what the exercise is, nor how long I do it. What matters is to do that one exercise I have chosen every day, more or less at the same time.

I have gone through many different exercise routines over the years. At one point it was a two-mile walk every morning. Another time it was calisthenics. Now, it is Kundalini Yoga in the morning, and Chi Gong in the evening.

There are rules to doing the same exercise day after day. The first rule is that the exercise must not cause pain. It is perfectly all right to go into a certain depth of discomfort. It is not acceptable to go into pain!

The second rule is to breathe. Become aware of your breathing, and adapt it to your exercise. When I was young, my father even knew that,

(-; and taught me to either breathe in for four steps and out for four, or in for eight breaths and out for eight.

The third rule, although this is optional, is to be heard. Make a noise while breathing. Chant a mantra, sing a hymn, groan aloud, or sigh. Do whatever comes up from your deepest inner self. Get rid of anger, let out grief, and open repressed feelings. Breathe the repressed feelings out, and breathe in love and compassion for yourself. Once you empty your cup of grief and replace it with compassion, you will be ready to share your love and compassion with others.

I am a great fan of the thirteenth century poet, Rumi. I indulged myself to attend two celebrations of his 800th birthday in 2005 and traveled to Ann Arbor, Michigan, to hear Robert Bly and Coleman Barks, my two favorite translators/poets read Rumi's work to a background of music. I also met Hosain Mosavat, an Iranian Sufi poet and became his student. I developed a set of conversations between Rumi and myself. One of these conversations, written in 2005, was about grief and compassion:

From Grief to Compassion

Rumi said,
"I saw grief drinking a cup of sorrow."
(Translated by Coleman Barks. Used with permission)

I asked grief,
"What will you teach me?"
And grief answered,
"To accept loss."
I asked again,
"What is it that I would learn from loss?"
And grief answered me what I already knew,
"Whatever it is you lost was not yours to begin with."

"Then why should I grieve at all?" I asked defiantly.
"Why should I drink a cup of sorrow?"

But grief reminded me,

"It is not you, but I, who drinks a cup of sorrow! Once you accept loss you also lose me and replace grief with compassion."

The ancient 'Hermetic' rule set the parameters of balance: "As above, so below. As inside, so outside."

What About My Mind?

Part 1: What's in My Mind?

My mind is constantly active. James Joyce proved this when he wrote his stream-of-consciousness novels, such as *Ulysses*. Dr. Joe Dispenza put it this way, and I paraphrase: 'all that internal chatter has been put there by me. It may have taken years, even decades, but I kept telling myself, or thinking every thought and word that is going on in my mind. I am responsible for it.'

So here is one area of adult behavior where taking responsibility is acceptable. It is clear that what I am not responsible for are all the things that happened to me. I am not responsible for all the things I learned, and all the emotions I repressed as a child. Any person who is over 25, whose pre-frontal lobe has developed, does have an opportunity to take responsibility, however. No, there are no instructions manuals (yet) on how to do that. My next book, *Responsible? Well..., Maybe,* will attempt to do that. But to 'grow up', means to stop being manipulated by the hurt child within.

My mind is ruled by the pain of the hurt child. There is a high probability that all the internal chatter of my mind consists of complaints about what's wrong with the world, what's wrong with other people, and/ or how ashamed and guilty I feel. All that is the stuff of an adult mind ruled by a hurt child. All that chatter in my mind is an attempt to cover up my emotional pain. All the useless conversations we have about 'look at what happened to me' are ways of soothing our pain.

If I put it there, I can take it out and replace it!

What About My Mind?

Part 2: The War I Tried to Avoid For So Long

Actually, I cannot take out what is in my mind. I have to replace it. I have to begin with purposefully choosing mantras, or sayings, or whatever it is that I *want* to be thinking about. It is work.

A curious pseudo-survival battle develops in my mind even as I begin this 'house-cleaning'. The existing 'garbage', that useless drivel of denigrating judgments and foolish opinions I have collected over a lifetime, begin to take on a collective will of their own.

You have heard of GIGO: "Garbage In Garbage Out." It doesn't work. My mind does not have a garbage shoot. Nobody has developed a mental garbage pick-up technique. The fears and angers of my hurt child are so strong, that I have to deal with each manipulation one by one. I have to invite that hurt child to trust me to love him/her, to trust me to surround him/her with love and compassion, and to enter my adult world of self-acceptance and self-confidence.

There are other ways. Thousands of other ways. One acquaintance of mine dances through her pain, replacing whatever her subconscious mind holds with the beauty and ecstasy that dance produces.

In a sense, the classic 'devil by my left ear' and 'angel by my right ear' battle begins. My inner 'garbage' has come to life, organized a survival plan and arranged itself in a battle formation against change. It is a perfectly natural process. Every time I want to get up early and do my morning exercises, a perfectly timed and very cleverly expressed disclaimer/objection comes up.

"You need your eight hours of sleep. You have only slept six and a half. You ain't no sleeping beauty, but you will benefit from another hour's sleep. You will likely not have time for an afternoon nap. The carpenter is here and will be drilling and hammering, building your back deck. Go back to sleep while you can."

I feel like a fool, getting up at the crack of dawn, bleary eyed, groggy, and listless. The voice of reason is right on. Everything it says rings true. Why fight it? I will try again tomorrow.

It doesn't work that way!

It is not a fight. It is not really a war. The reasoning aspect of my mind, being dualistic, seems to seize upon and enjoy controversy, confrontation, challenge, competition, and especially winning. But the same reason offers the challenge of replacing negative, judgmental and unconscious responses to my environment with open-minded, curious, educational thought patterns. The subconscious mind is totally habituated. Habits are mostly unconscious. The medulla and the amygdala are hell-bent on keeping the status quo. That is their natural function.

With their help, my beliefs and opinions have closed my mind. I am not learning anything. I am only confirming what I already know.

Although such confirmation makes me feel good, I remain the same dumb-ass I have always been. Of course, as long as I don't know (am not aware) that my beliefs, opinions, and one-sided perspectives are keeping me dumbed down, I also don't know that I may be acting foolishly, saying irrational things, and living with a high degree of self-sabotage.

OK, it is not a war. It is a matter of self-motivation.

I have to make that decision to learn. No one is going to make it for me. I have to motivate myself, or go and attend a course that will urge me to motivate myself!

This is not the end. Changing a habit, facing a pain, and releasing a trauma all take much work. My Compassionate Inquiry Practice is a two-way street. I may create a safe place for others to look at their pain, but I see my own at the same time. How that works for both of us, and what possibilities there are for taking responsibility will, indeed, be another book.

CPSIA information can be obtained
at www.ICGtesting.com
Printed in the USA
BVHW031048141119
563830BV00001B/45/P

9 781982 235130